C000138367

Before the throne of God above

of God above

Jesus: our heavenly High Priest

© Day One Publications 2004
First printed 2004

ISBN 1 903087 59-7

Scripture quotations are from The New International Version unless otherwise stated.
© 1973, 1978, 1984, International Bible Society. Published by Hodder and Stoughton

British Library Cataloguing in Publication Data available

Published by Day One Publications
P O Box 66, Leominster, HR6 0XB
01568 613 740 FAX 01568 611 473

email—sales@dayone.co.uk
web site—www.dayone.co.uk
North American—e-mail-sales@dayonebookstore.com
North American web site—www.dayonebookstore.com

All rights reserved
No part of this publication may be reproduced, or stored in a retrieval system, or
transmitted, in any form or by any means, mechanical, electronic, photocopying,
recording or otherwise, without the prior permission of Day One Publications.

Designed by Steve Devane and printed by CPD

Dedication

To Rev. Alan Tovey MA BD (1942–2002).
As General Secretary of the Evangelical Fellowship of Congregational
Churches he organised the sabbatical during which this book took shape,
provided constructive criticism when it was written
and encouraged its publication.
The hymn, which provides the title to this book, was chosen by him to be
sung at his funeral.

Before the throne of God above

Before the throne of God above
I have a strong, a perfect plea,
A great High Priest, whose Name is Love,
Who ever lives and pleads for me.

My name is graven on his hands,
My name is written on his heart;
I know that while in heaven he stands,
No tongue can bid me hence depart.

When Satan tempts me to despair,
And tells me of the wrong within,
Upward I look to see him there
Who made an end of all my sin.

Because the sinless Saviour died,
My sinful soul is counted free;
For God the Just is satisfied
To look on him, and pardon me.

Behold him there! the risen Lamb!
My perfect, spotless righteousness,
The great, unchangeable I AM,
The King of glory and of grace!

One with himself I cannot die,
My soul is purchased by his blood;
My life is hid with Christ on high,
With Christ, my Saviour and my God.

Charitie Lees de Chenez (1841–1923)

Contents

Foreword

I have been acquainted with Michael Plant since 1986 when we met in Uckfield, England for the formation of the World Evangelical Congregational Fellowship, but we have been friends since 2000 when we were on sabbatical together at Westminster College in Cambridge. While I focused on the English Reformation, Michael worked long and hard on his study of the Book of Hebrews. Though our conversations did not generally centre in our respective areas of study, I found Michael to always have the ability to get to the heart of an issue, and to speak to it with reason and conviction.

It was a delight, but no surprise, then, to read this pastoral commentary on Hebrews, and to find it marked by clear thinking and practical insight. This is not a verse-by-verse commentary, but rather a presentation of Jesus Christ as our great High Priest. Michael argues that Hebrews was written for Jewish Christians who were scattered, discouraged and tempted to abandon their new found faith, and that Jesus Christ was presented to them as a sympathetic High Priest who could help them, primarily through his ministry of intercession based on his finished work on the cross.

Christians today are not unlike those to whom Hebrews was addressed. Fear, loneliness and rejection still tempt Christians in all parts of the world to question, doubt and forsake their faith because of various types of persecution and abuse. What they often need is a clear understanding of Christ's priestly office. This is a very practical exposition, then, for Christians who suffer or are discouraged, which includes all of us at various times in our Christian walk.

In a day when theology is denigrated, even in Christian circles, this book is an important reminder that theology, or correct thinking about God, is of great practical benefit for the living of the Christian life.

Drawing from his own experience, Michael writes with both understanding and conviction. His approach is both scholarly and pastoral. Reading this book will provide the reader, not only with information, but with encouragement and hope.

CLIFFORD CHRISTENSEN, CONFERENCE MINISTER OF THE CONSERVATIVE CONGREGATIONAL CHRISTIAN CONFERENCE (USA) 1981–2003

How and why this book came to be written

In the first three months of 2000 I had the privilege of a Cheshunt Foundation Sabbatical at Westminster College, Cambridge. I wanted to pursue my special interest in the book of Hebrews with a study and writing project. Initially I took up a suggestion of the Person of Christ in Hebrews but quickly decided that to have a manageable project I must narrow this down to the portrait of Christ as High Priest. This is a theme which I believe has great value.

THE PASTORAL VALUE OF THIS THEME

I remember one lady, who subsequently died of cancer, finding a sermon on Hebrews 5:7–10 very helpful in a time of special need. It gave her a new realization of the reality of the humanity and suffering of the Lord Jesus and so helped her cope with her own suffering. Another lady, who had problems with assurance of salvation, was helped by a hymn I copied out for her. The hymn was, 'Before the throne of God above', from which the title of this book is taken. I chose this particular hymn because I had found it so encouraging in my own times of difficulty.

THE TIMELINESS OF THIS THEME

Particular truths of God's word, like the doctrine of justification at the Reformation, can have a great impact on a generation because that specific truth speaks deeply to the particular needs of Christians at that time. These truths concerning Jesus as High Priest were formulated and recorded for Christians under pressure in an alien world and tempted to give up on their faith. For many Christians today, in the secularised Western world as well as in areas where Christians suffer overt persecution, this is a familiar scenario.

It was a great joy at Keswick 1999 to find the hymn put to a new and modern setting and being warmly received by those who had not previously known it. Perhaps it will be a good time to explore this theme in more detail and depth in order to encourage the Lord's people.

MY PERSONAL APPRECIATION OF THIS THEME

The Hebrew Christians to whom this letter was written were clearly facing major discouragements and a decrease in the numbers meeting together. Understandably, if wrongly, they felt like giving up. This is why they needed the assurance of a sympathetic high priest who was able to bring help to them. Though the reasons were very different, being mainly due to bereavements and people moving for employment reasons, the church I was pastoring had experienced considerable decline at the time I wrote this book. Both the temptation to give up and the comfort and help of Jesus our sympathetic High Priest have been realities to me. They enabled me to persevere until God in his goodness brought us through that difficult period in the church's life to a time of great encouragement.

Our way of approach

THE IMPORTANCE OF A PASTORAL APPROACH

Many of the problems in understanding Hebrews diminish considerably with the realization that it was written to deal with pastoral difficulties, which were so severe that the Hebrew Christians were tempted to abandon their faith. When we see how Christians have responded to these truths in their praise and worship we actually gain valuable insights into how to understand Hebrews. The writers of older hymns, which are frequently quoted, have often grasped spiritual riches from the text that can become valuable to us. It would be good if more contemporary hymn writers took up these themes and I would be delighted if this book encourages them to do so.

AN OUTLINE OF THE BOOK

The first two chapters of this book will explore the pastoral needs Hebrews sets out to meet and the way in which it meets them. The next eight chapters will explore the subject of the High Priesthood of Christ by taking the description of the High Priest and his tasks and qualifications in Hebrews

5:1–3 as our basis. We will major on the teaching about Christ's sympathy and his intercession for us as our high priest. This is the teaching that lies at the heart of the message of the letter. As we explore the way in which Jesus is now interceding for us in heaven, we will look at what the gospels tell us about his intercession for his disciples on earth. John 17 and other incidents show our Saviour giving us a preview on earth of what he is now doing for us in heaven. The final chapter will link us to our brothers and sisters in Christ who down the years have been sustained and strengthened by these truths.

Acknowledgements

I am profoundly grateful to the Cheshunt Foundation for providing the funds and a great deal of academic support during my sabbatical. My thanks also go to my family, Margaret, David and Jonathan, and to the officers and members of Cannon Park Congregational Church, Middlesbrough for allowing me the time to be away from them.

Problems and pastoral response (1)

Once you do know what the question actually is, you'll know what the answer means

Hebrews is a book of answers that demand questions to go with them. In 'The Hitchhiker's Guide to the Galaxy', the computer Deep Thought comes up with the answer to the Great Question of Life, the Universe and Everything. The answer is Forty-two. Everyone complains at this anticlimax to which the computer replies, 'I think the problem, to be quite honest with you, is that you've never actually known what the problem is … So once you do know what the question actually is, you'll know what the answer means.'[1] If you read through the book of Hebrews you will find little difficulty in working out what the writer believes is the answer to the problems faced by the Hebrew Christians. It is that they need to gain an understanding and appreciation of Jesus as their great High Priest. However because this concept is based on the Old Testament pattern of life and worship, it is alien to us as 21st century Christians and so people find Hebrews difficult and unrewarding, and fail to appreciate the answer. To help us avoid this we will first examine the problems that lie behind the writing of Hebrews in order fully to understand and benefit from the answer that Hebrews gives us.

Christ is the answer

No one who reads the letter to the Hebrews could doubt for a minute that the writer sees Christ as the answer to the needs of those to whom he is writing. This is clear from the very first verses of chapter one, which acts as an introduction to the whole letter. Without any greetings section, such as we would find in most of the letters of the New Testament, the writer contrasts the present, 'in these last days [God] has spoken to us by his Son' (v 2), with the entire past period of Old Testament revelation, 'In the past God spoke to our forefathers at many times and in various ways' (v 1). The contrasts are firstly between the once for all nature of God speaking to us in a Son and the long periods and different types of speech used before. Secondly, in the fact that this event brings in a new era in God's dealings with humanity, 'these last days' (v 2). William Lane translates the expression as, 'this final age',[2] which is the period when decisive events that fulfil the Old Testament promises of God's triumph through his Messiah have taken place. These are the D-Day events that guarantee the eventual VE day of complete and final triumph when all God's promises in Christ will have been fulfilled.

The reason for these contrasts between the two periods of revelation is the greatness of the Son. This greatness is seen in his involvement in the creation of the universe, 'through whom he made the universe'; in its continuance, 'sustaining all things by his powerful word'; and in its destiny, 'whom he appointed heir of all things.' Also in that he is intimately related to God as 'the radiance of God's glory and the exact representation of his being' and that he is one who has dealt with sin completely, in a way no other has done before him; 'After he had provided purification for sins, he sat down at the right hand of the majesty in heaven.'

This emphasis on Christ as the answer continues throughout the letter. There are direct commands: 'fix your thoughts on Jesus, the apostle and high priest whom we confess' (3:1), and: 'Let us fix our eyes on Jesus, the author and perfecter of our faith' (12:2) and there is detailed and lengthy teaching on Jesus as 'our great high priest who has gone through the heavens' (4:14). This teaching about Jesus as a great High Priest is developed in the passage from 4:14 to 10:31. This is the subject that will be the focus of this book. What we need to do at the outset of our study is to consider what problems those receiving this letter had and what questions they needed answering.

The danger the Hebrews are in
We can advance our understanding by looking at the evident danger that confronted those receiving the letter. One of the major features of the letter to the Hebrews is the warning passages. Without going into detail about the

interpretation of these passages, which I have done elsewhere,[3] there are certain points that are obvious. These are people who have heard and received the truth and whose danger is that they may 'drift away' (2:1) and who therefore in their faith and life need to 'hold firmly to the end the confidence we had at first' (3:14). The result of a failure at this point would be catastrophic for those receiving the letter. If 'we ignore such a great salvation' (2:3), then there is only 'a fearful expectation of judgement and of raging fire' (10:27).

A particular cause of concern here is that the Hebrew Christians do not realise their danger. This is why Hebrews 3:13 warns them of the danger of being 'hardened by sin's deceitfulness.' Sin, even the major sin of deserting the gospel and hardening the heart against God, never appears in its true colours. Sin deceives us both as to its nature and its consequences. One 17th century writer says, 'All the devices of sin are as fair baits whereby dangerous hooks are covered over to entice silly fish to snap at them, so as they are taken and made a prey to the fisher.'[4]

Clearly then we are not so much looking at a particular temptation or problem within the Christian life. What is warned against is the danger of actually deserting the Christian gospel and so abandoning a Christian lifestyle and coming under God's judgement.

The questions and problems facing the Hebrews

There are a number of these and most of them link to the identity of the group of Christians receiving the letter. I am taking the view, with the majority of scholars, that the recipients are Christians with a Jewish background and are members of the dispersion, that is, that the Jewish communities to which they belong are not in Palestine but are among those dispersed around the Mediterranean world. The evidence that the audience is Jewish is that the argument of the letter deals largely with Jewish institutions and practices, which would be a strange method to adopt if one were writing to non-Jews. The evidence that they are Jews of the dispersion is shown by the use of the Septuagint for quotations. The Septuagint was the Greek version of the Old Testament used in the synagogues of the dispersion. Some writers are more specific in terms of the group's background, thinking for example of a group of former priests or those who have an Essene background. This speculation completely outruns any evidence we have. The same applies to the attempt to be dogmatic about the location of the congregation—for example locating them in Rome. Whatever disagreements there may be about questions like these it is actually far more important that we grasp the external and internal difficulties these Christians were facing. These are matters that the text of Hebrews does give us great help with.

Problem 1: suffering for the faith

Both when the writer to the Hebrews talks about the past: 'Remember those earlier days after you had received the light, when you stood your ground in a great contest in the face of suffering' (10:32) and the present: 'In your struggle against sin, you have not yet resisted to the point of shedding your blood' (12:4), he is realistic about the experiences they have had and may yet face. They had stood firm in the past: 'Sometimes you were publicly exposed to insult and persecution; and at other times you stood side by side with those who were so treated. You sympathised with those in prison and joyfully accepted the confiscation of your property, because you knew that you yourselves had better and lasting possessions' (10:33–34). They need to continue to do so but the danger is they may 'shrink back' (10:39). Though it is not made explicit in the letter it seems probable that the shrinking back would be to turn from the Christian faith to Judaism, which was a tolerated religion in the Roman Empire. The Jews had exemption from practices such as Emperor worship, which were no less unacceptable to the Christian community.

We can all sympathise with the Hebrew Christians because most of us can cope with difficulties and suffering, such as nastiness from family members or from colleagues at work, for a short time. Our problem really comes when there is no let up in hostilities as time goes by and no sign that there ever will be. Once I had a job in a garage and part of the cost of being a Christian was to make a stand against the unpleasant and overt racism of some of the staff. This I did and suffered considerable hostility as a result. To make that initial stand against racism was hard but I found that in the longer term the temptation to compromise in other less obvious areas was greater. This was because compromise on other matters meant I could escape the prospect of long-drawn out antagonism in my workplace. The Hebrew Christians likewise found the long-term problems of suffering for their faith more difficult than the short term ones.

Problem 2: The problem of not belonging

When shopping for trainers I worry about comfort and price. I am middle-aged and do not even know which labels are acceptable at the moment. My 17–year-old son looks for labels. If a product does not have the right label then it does not even get considered. It is not that comfort and price do not bother him, but whether or not he is seen as fitting in with his friends and what they wear worries him a lot more. Understandably we all like a sense of belonging.

It is a sense of belonging that the Hebrew Christians are desperately missing. There are several reasons for this; firstly it is because of estrangement from the Jewish Community and the practice of the Jewish faith. In this period the Jewish community was not in a ghetto, as it was so often later on, but still formed a strong, distinct and united group. As time went on the Christian community, in some areas still largely Jewish, was progressively cut off from the Jewish community. Gordon J Keddie writes:

The ties of nation and family, of sentiment and tradition, all constitute a siren call for Hebrew Christians and their modern equivalent, the Messianic Jews. For Jewish Christians, the fact that the Old Testament patterns for worship and life had been God's mandate made it all the more difficult to come to the place of seeing certain parts of it fall away because Messiah had come.5

Their desire for belonging surfaces in the way in which the writer to the Hebrews encourages them. They feel cut off from Jerusalem, the city which forms a centre of Jewish life and worship, so they are encouraged that by the example of Abraham, who also left his roots, and was: 'looking forward to the city with foundations, whose architect and builder is God' (11:10). In the same way, Abraham's descendants, who are identified with the Christian community in 2:16, are 'longing for a better country—a heavenly one. Therefore God is not ashamed to be called their God, for he has prepared a city for them' (11:16). They actually have already: 'come to

Mount Zion, to the heavenly Jerusalem, the city of the living God' (12:22). Jesus also suffered rejection by the Jewish people and 'suffered outside the city gate to make the people holy through his own blood' (Hebrews 13:12). Their responsibility is to respond in faith and to 'go to him [Jesus] outside the camp, bearing the disgrace he bore. For here we do not have an enduring city, but we are looking for the city that is to come' (13:13-14).

Another factor in this may be the problem of loss within the Christian community. People are exhorted, 'Let us not give up meeting together, as some are in the habit of doing' (10:25) and so clearly have seen a falling away from the group of believers they meet with. In the first two centuries of Christianity there were no special buildings used for worship and believers would meet together in the home of one of the members. When, in the third century, special buildings were constructed for Christian gatherings, they were modelled on the room into which guests were received in the typical Roman or Greek household. This clearly put a limit on the number who could meet, for such a room could accommodate thirty people in comfort and perhaps half as many again in discomfort. This would mean that, if the Hebrew Christians' meeting followed a typical pattern, the group was probably no larger, and possibly smaller, than 45.[6] This would mean that even a small number of believers leaving the fellowship would be very noticeable, and very discouraging to those who remain. Recently a family of seven, who can make up nearly a quarter of our evening congregation, joined our church. Then later we lost a family of four due to a sudden and serious illness. To gain or lose even a small number is very noticeable in a small group of people. Additionally they have lost, perhaps through persecution, their first generation of leaders (13:7). Often when strong leaders leave a church or a Christian organisation, some believers, who previously appeared quite stable and reliable, begin to waver in their commitment and to lose confidence. It is for this reason that they are reminded to, 'Consider the outcome of their [your leaders'] way of life and imitate their faith' (13:7) and are reminded that, 'Jesus Christ [the focus of that faith] is the same, yesterday and today and for ever' (13:8). Certainly these factors of experienced loss will contribute to making the Hebrew Christians feel alone and rather helpless as events go on.

Chapter 1

Problem 3: Weaknesses in their own faith

When we experience problems, as Christians there are nearly always external difficulties involved. Things that are happening, or not happening, precipitate the problems. However, the reason that these external difficulties become problems is most often because of internal defects in our own faith and understanding. There does appear to be such a defect in the faith of the Hebrew Christians. Its nature can be deduced from the way in which the writer stresses the inwardness and non-visibility of the truths of the Christian faith throughout the letter. These aspects point to its superiority, that it is 'better' as the writer often expresses it, when compared to what went before. One example of this is in 9:11–14, where Christ 'went through the greater and more perfect tabernacle that is not man-made, that is to say not a part of this creation' (v 11). The place then is heaven and the sacrifice is not the visible repetitive sacrifice of 'the blood of goats and calves' but 'his own blood' (v 12) once offered in the past on Calvary. The result is not that the sacrifice will 'sanctify them so that they are outwardly clean' (v 13), but that it will 'cleanse our consciences ... so that we may serve the living God' (v 14). This stress results from the fulfilment, not the abolition, of the Old Testament pattern of worship and sacrifice, which takes place in Christ. Clearly it appears that the Hebrew Christians actually missed and regretted the loss of the outward and visible aspects, the ceremonies and sacrifices, associated with Old Covenant worship and were not enjoying the full cleansing of conscience that the gospel offered to them.

The problem of relying too much on visible things is clearly being guarded against in Hebrews 10:35–11:40. The section aims to inspire to faith by the example of faithful heroes but there is a deeper message about faith which needs to be appreciated as well. Faith is 'being sure of what we hope for and certain of what we do not see' (11:1). Looking through the chapter we realise that the common link is that faith bases itself on God's promises and not on anything visible or touchable. This is still how Christians are to live although we are living at a later stage in the fulfilment of God's plans and promises; 'God had planned something better for us so that only together with us would they be made perfect' (11:40). This flagging of faith experienced by the Hebrew Christians is not anything else than failing to believe God. In the 21st century, like the first, we experience the problem of continuing in faith when events and disappointments disillusion and discourage us. Almost never are people persuaded out of their Christian commitment by argument. Almost always difficulty and discouragement erode them out of it.

However in Hebrews 13:9–16 there is a direct reference to the problem, although the details must be regarded as obscure. What the Hebrew Christians must not do is to seek for their 'hearts to be strengthened ... by ceremonial foods, which are of no value to those who eat them' (v 9). In contrast, 'it is good for our hearts to be strengthened by grace'. The likelihood is that the ceremonial foods are connected with the Jewish sacrifices but, though this and other details are debatable, the key point is plain. Christianity is not primarily a religion of ceremonial and sacrament but of faith in Jesus resulting in a way of life lived in response to his sacrifice. A recent commentator writes that the Christian faith, as taught to the Hebrew Christians is a 'piety that is not grounded in sacramental practice, but that draws directly from the sacrificial death of Christ implications for the Christian life.'[7] Geerhardus Vos, who believes that the recipients of the letter were Gentile Christians, writes, 'the hypothesis of religious externalism lying at the bottom of the readers' trouble seems to explain their condition.'[8] Externalism is a desire to feel and handle things and have them as supports to our faith. This is felt to be an easier option than living by a faith based on God's word and promise alone. This meant that their experience of humiliation on the way to glory, and the delay in the fulfilment of all God's promises in Christ, presented them with a persistent and nagging problem.

There is nothing remote about this problem and the Lord Jesus warned his disciples in the Parable of the Sower (Matthew 13:1–23) that some believers will last 'only a short time. [Because] When trouble or persecution comes because of the word, he quickly falls away' (v 21). In other words such 'believers' cannot live by faith when faced with serious and painful difficulties. A similar problem has shown itself in recent years when several prominent evangelicals, such as Thomas Howard and Franky Schaeffer, have joined the Roman Catholic and Orthodox churches. One factor motivating the decision has been the need to join a visible Christian community with historic roots in face of the gimmickry and pragmatic nature of much contemporary evangelicalism. An emphasis on ceremony and historical tradition like this can be misleading to us, as the continuity we need to seek is spiritual and relates to shared faith rather than institutions and ceremonies. Peter Adam writes:

Hebrews asserts that, in the words of the writer of the preface concerning ceremonies in the Book of Common Prayer, 'Christ's Gospel is not Ceremonial Law (as much of Moses' Law was) but it is a Religion to serve God, not in bondage of figure or shadow, but in the freedom of the Spirit. 'Christianity is not a cultic religion. Our ever-stronger emphasis on the beautiful traditions of Anglican worship (and other liturgical traditions) may be obscuring this truth in practise today. 9

The great emphasis in recent years on spirituality and spiritualities, which in many ways can be very helpful, does run the risk of falling into this error.

Moving on

So far, then, we have looked at the problems experienced by the Hebrew Christians for which the major answer is Christ as our great High Priest. In the next chapter we will begin to explore the way in which the writer to the Hebrews answers the questions raised by the troubles of those to whom he writes.

Notes

1 **Douglas Adams,** The Hitchhiker's Guide to the Galaxy—A Trilogy in Four Parts, Heinemann, 1986, pp. 128–129. The use of this wonderfully apposite quotation indicates no sympathy with the author's clear anti-theistic slant.

2 **William Lane,** Word Bible Commentary Hebrews 1–8, p. 5.

3 **Michael Plant,** Foundations, Spring 1993, No. 30, pp. 11–19.

4 **William Gouge,** cited in **A W Pink,** An Exposition of Hebrews, Baker, 1954 (1971 Reprint), p. 181.

5 **Gordon J Keddie,** The Practical Christian—James Simply Explained, Evangelical Press, p. 220.

6 **Robert Banks,** Paul's Idea of Community, Paternoster, 1980, pp. 40–42.

7   **H W Attridge,** *Hermeneia Commentary on Hebrews,* SCM/Fortress, p. 390.
8   **Geerhardus Vos,** *The Teaching of the Epistle to the Hebrews,* Eerdmans, 1956, p. 21.
9   **Peter Adam,** *The Majestic Son,* Anglican Information Office, 1992, p. 153.

Problems and pastoral response (2)

Think of our Lord as priest, and I will make you understand.[1]

A friend of mine described the first time he read the Puritan John Owen. He was sitting on a bus travelling to a student conference and as he read the rather difficult and uninspiring prose he suddenly realised why it was that so many people were highly recommending this writer. He came to a realisation; 'This man knows me' and it is this quality of discerning what is going on inside us that characterises the Bible and writers such as Owen, who have meditated long and deep on the teaching of the Bible. Whether four or twenty centuries separate us from other Christians, we have fundamentally the same problems as they did and the solutions are also the same. So, before we begin to look in detail at the theme of the Priesthood of Christ we need to pursue further our investigation of the problems faced by the Hebrew Christians. We have looked at them in an objective way and considered their historical situation and problems. However, what inward effects did the problems and situations they faced have on them? What particular difficulties arose when their expectations and attitudes were brought into contact with the gospel? This is not something remote from us because, like them, we can all become disillusioned and begin to struggle in our Christian walk.

Jews encounter Jesus

CAN THIS REALLY BE THE MESSIAH?

When the apostle Paul looked at the world scene into which he was proclaiming the gospel there were two factors at work in his response. Firstly there was his desire to proclaim the gospel clearly. A comparison of his sermons, in a synagogue (Acts 13:16–41), to unsophisticated and superstitious pagans (Acts 14:14–17) and to sophisticated and arrogant intellectuals (Acts 17:22–31), shows clearly how he adapts to preaching in different situations. The second factor is his frank acknowledgement that his message is a difficult one for people to accept and that without the Spirit's power at work they will not do so. Paul's mission statement is: 'but we preach Christ crucified: a stumbling block to Jews and foolishness to Gentiles' (1 Corinthians 1:23). Each new situation where the gospel is heard will have its own points of offence and resistance. We can sharpen the impact of this message to a Jewish hearer by supplying another expanded translation and interpretation, 'we preach Messiah as having been crucified and therefore accursed by God.'

In Jewish thinking there would come a day when God would intervene in this world's affairs through his Messiah. Before this date God's people were humiliated and suffered and then they would be triumphant because vindicated and honoured by God. There are then two ages and the second one will follow on from and replace the first. The Christian gospel alters this neat scheme. The two ages overlap and the last days (of the present age) are days in which the final triumph still awaits but in which the decisive events which guarantee this have already taken place. Jesus has died, has risen, is glorified and will come again in triumph. But suffering and humiliation, as the way to glory, characterised his life on earth and will characterise his people's life experience as well. Much of the New Testament is devoted to this problem and the apostolic follow-up is blunt and honest, 'We must go through many hardships to enter the kingdom of God' (Acts 14: 22). It is worth checking whether our follow up courses for new Christians do mention that, 'everyone who wants to live a godly life in Christ Jesus will be persecuted' (2 Timothy 3:12).

There can be no doubt that the Hebrew Christians struggled with this problem. They needed not only to know that hardship was inevitable as a facet of Christian experience but also to understand the reason for it. This is why the writer assures them, 'In bringing many sons to glory it was fitting that God, for whom and through whom everything exists, should make the author of their salvation perfect through suffering' (2:10). The point being made is that the same wisdom displayed by God in creating the world for his own glory is being displayed by God in the humiliation and suffering of his Messiah. How can Jesus save those who are 'being tempted' (2:18) and 'held in slavery by their fear of death' (2:15), without being one who 'shared in their humanity' (2:14) and was 'made like his brothers in every way' (2:17). What this means is that the experience of frailty is not surprising to them or inappropriate for Jesus calls them, 'the children God has given me' (2:13 quoting Isaiah 8:18). Jesus' relationship with Christians is based on his becoming a real human being and sharing all our experiences of suffering and so in our sufferings we can always be grateful that our saviour walked the same pathway before us.

WHAT DID IT FEEL LIKE FOR THESE JEWS TO BE CHRISTIANS?
William Lane very movingly and with great insight describes the quandary of the Hebrew Christians and the pastoral response of the writer in his letter:

Social alienation and persecution encourage one to doubt the willingness or power of God to act in the present ... Doubt in the ability of God to act would appear to be closely associated with doubt that he had acted definitively in Christ. The writer's pastoral task was to help the community realize the reality of God's decisive action in Christ and of Christ's present ability to act on their behalf ... His strongest encouragement was to remind the members of the house church of the character, the accomplishment, and the exalted status of their Lord.[2]

Here is described accurately what we often experience. When family and personal problems overwhelm us and God seems far away it is very hard to appreciate and respond positively to the great truths of the gospel because they seem remote. So also do the warnings of scripture about judgement on sin; a factor that may be reflected in the strength of the warning passages in Hebrews. The end result of such experiences can be that we become disappointed and hurt and retreat from our faith commitment to Jesus. Lane's analysis of the problem can be summarised:—
i The problem arises because God has not acted in the present to dispel the suffering of the Hebrew Christians.
ii The current experience of God not intervening weakens faith in what he has already done through Christ and his cross.

iii The answer is to rebuild faith in what God has done through Christ. Through this rebuilding of faith in Christ's finished work we will find that faith in God's power to save and help in the present may also be revived.

What answers does the writer to the Hebrews have?

THERE ARE NO SIMPLE SOLUTIONS

The upshot of all this is that the problems of the Hebrew Christians do not have easy and direct solutions. An illustration of this can be drawn from events at a recent Commonwealth Games. It was often pointed out that the Australian swimming team showed great loyalty to one another and that those not swimming would always be there to cheer on their compatriots. A great deal of their success was attributed to this encouragement. However one Australian swimmer had previously been world class in one particular stroke but had lost the ability to swim competitively. She had to compete in another event because this difficulty would not be helped by being cheered on but by taking time out to completely rebuild that stroke. Likewise the Hebrew Christians do not simply need a little encouragement but to have their faith rebuilt by building on the foundation of faith they have. Peter Adam writes: 'Hebrews assumes that the best form of Christian encouragement is a strong dose of theology and Bible teaching. Perhaps our attempts at encouraging one another are a bit thin in comparison!'[3]

WHY GO DOWN THE ROAD OF THIS TEACHING ABOUT JESUS AS HIGH PRIEST?

Why does the writer to the Hebrews choose to major on the High Priesthood of the Lord Jesus? There are other themes the letter touches on but this is the central and dominating theme. William Lane writes: 'By assigning the centre to the exposition of Jesus as exalted priest, the dominant notion is that of sustained care, and ... encourages an attitude of confident trust.'[4]

Help comes as the Hebrew Christians are brought to realize that Jesus has not only dealt with sin once for all but also that he is now in heaven as one who knows the reality of living a life of faith amidst temptation and so is able to send them help and support. JH Thornwell grasps the essence of the movement in their faith from Judaism to Christianity. It is not that they cease to believe in the covenant faithfulness of God but that: 'The covenant faithfulness of God is seen to be maintained through the agency of him who ever liveth to make intercession for us.'[5]

The theme of Christ's high priesthood is open to the writer because it pursues an Old Testament link made by Jesus in the gospels (Matthew 22:44 and parallels) and by Peter in his sermon at Pentecost (Acts 2:35). They both refer to Psalm 110:1, 'The LORD says to my Lord: "Sit at my right hand until I make your enemies a footstool for your feet."' It is the most frequently used Old Testament passage for explaining the Messiah-ship of Jesus. However what the writer of Hebrews is unique in doing is linking what is clearly a psalm about the Messiah with the idea of a new priesthood as in Psalm 110:4, 'The LORD has sworn and will not change his mind: "You are a priest for ever, in the order of Melchizedek"' It is not that the idea of a priestly ministry by Jesus does not exist elsewhere in the New Testament. Jesus is mentioned as intercessor in Romans 8:34 and as an advocate with the Father on the basis of his sacrifice in 1 John 2:1–2. Although the terms that indicate priestly activity are not used in John 17 it is appropriate, in view of its contents, that this part of scripture has for many years been described as Christ's High Priestly prayer. However, within the New Testament, the idea of Jesus as High Priest being developed in any detail is unique to Hebrews.

An outline of the letter to the Hebrews

How the book of Hebrews is structured is a difficult and perhaps insoluble problem. I am not attempting to give a complete outline but simply to highlight the letter's main themes. As to whether properly speaking Hebrews is a letter or not, I agree with the view that this 'word of exhortation' (13:22) is, as in Acts 13:16, a sermon. To this sermon the greetings at the end of Hebrews 13 have been added so it could be circulated in the form of a letter. To draw attention to Christ's High Priesthood as a major theme of Hebrews I have italicised the outline when this theme is to the fore.

1:1–3: Introductory statement summarising the main themes of the letter. The finality and superiority of God's revelation in Christ compared to the Old Covenant. Christ's greatness in relationship to God himself, to the universe and to *purification of sin. In this priestly task Jesus has been so successful as to end his work by sitting down.*

1:4–14: This passage deals with Christ's superiority over angels. The reason for this is that the giving of the law was associated with angels (2:2).

2:1–4: First warning passage. The gospel message brings both a greater salvation and a greater responsibility of obedience than the revelation of the law.

2:5–18: The subject of the letter is put in its broadest perspective. The destiny of mankind is to rule over the created order. This destiny is restored in and through Christ. In order that we might be raised to this salvation God chose to qualify Jesus through suffering to lead us to salvation. He can bring us salvation in temptations and fears because he has so shared our nature and situation as to understand them and be able to help us in them. *Here for the first time Jesus is called (merciful and faithful) High Priest.*

3:1–4:13: Here the writer explores the meaning of faithfulness. The heads of the two covenant communities, Moses and Jesus, were both faithful. However Moses' faithfulness was as a servant whose ministry served the future. Jesus is the Son to whom the house belongs. Like the Israelites in the desert we need to respond in faith to God's promise of rest. Active faith brings us to rest but disobedience means the word of God promising salvation will actually bring judgement.

4:14–5:10: For the first time the writer begins to develop his main theme. Because Jesus is Priest we can expect help in our temptations—particularly the temptation to abandon faith. In 5: 1–3 there are four essential points about High Priests—

Appointment by God.
Representing men to God
Offering gifts and sacrifices
The ability, through being able to sympathise, to help the weak.
These are fulfilled in Jesus and the theme of his ability to empathise with and help the weak is especially developed in 5:7–9.

5:11–6:20: A lengthy warning passage about the dangers of continuing spiritual immaturity. The danger is that we will instead fall away and will be lost. The readers are encouraged through the evidence of the reality of their faith and through the certainty of God's promise, given on oath, to continue in faith. The hope given to Christians focuses on *Jesus who is in God's presence as Priest for us.*

7:1–28: In vs 1–10 the writer talks about the historical figure of Melchizedek. This takes up the theme of appointment by God first announced in chapter five. Melchizedek is seen as one who brings blessing to God's people and who is greater than Levi, the ancestor of all the High Priests. *In vs 11–28 it is spelt out why Jesus is a Melchizedekean High Priest rather than a Levitical one. Both the quality of the salvation he brings and its permanency meets the needs of his people.*

8:1–10:18: Three subjects intermingle in this section. *The covenant of which Jesus is Priest, which is the New Covenant,* promising sins remembered no more and a closer knowledge of God, announced in Jeremiah 31:31–34. *The Tabernacle in which he serves is (9:24) 'Heaven itself'.* And *The offering he brings is the spiritual and rational offering of himself which achieved, in its once for all offering, all time forgiveness of sins and a status as holy for God's people.*

10:19–31: Encouragements to continue in faith and warnings not to defect based on the truths taught in the section above.

10:32–12:3: Encouragements to faith based on their own past experience, the past examples of Old Testament believers and the example of Jesus himself.

12:4–29: A series of encouragements and warnings drawn from the book of Proverbs, the history of Israel and of Esau, the spiritual realities involved in their faith and worship and the greater responsibility we have in hearing the new covenant message.

13:1–17: The rubber hits the road. Leaving the Christian faith normally comes about through practical disobedience rather than theoretical unbelief. The Hebrew Christians are warned about practical ways in which they may go astray (such as lovelessness, sexual impurity, discontentment, false worship and unruliness in church life).

13:18–25: Blessings and greetings.

Other themes in Hebrews
There are a number of other themes in Hebrews, which broaden the perspective the writer gives us on who Jesus is and what he has done. Often

these can be seen as linked to and coherent with the theme of Jesus as High Priest.

Christ as wisdom. For example it is suggested that the view of Christ in Hebrews 1:1–3 is heavily dependent on the wisdom literature of the Old Testament. Particularly the personification of wisdom in Proverbs 8:22–31, as well as on other Israelite wisdom literature not in the Bible, such as 'The Wisdom of Solomon.' It is certainly possible to see the personalised figure of wisdom, which acts as an intermediary between God and creation as foreshadowing the Christ who is the mediator of the new creation.

Christ the author of salvation and faith. An important title of Christ is that of the 'author of their salvation' (2:10), and, 'the author ... of our faith' (12:2). Geerhardus Vos writes that the author of salvation, 'is the one who leads others unto salvation by himself treading the path of salvation before', and the author of faith, 'is one who leads others to faith by himself exercising faith in an ideal manner.'[6] Again this fits well with the idea of Jesus as High Priest representing his people and leading them into the holy of holies.

Christ and our worship. A problem many small congregations may face is depression and a feeling of worthlessness and insignificance when they gather to worship. Hebrews has the cure because another important theme is the significance of the gathered and worshipping community. We perhaps would think firstly of the command in 10:25, 'Let us not give up meeting together, as some are in the habit of doing' but to appreciate this theme we need to realize the promises Jesus makes about the gathering of his people. As they sit together in the congregation to hear the letter read they hear these words from Jesus, 'I will declare your name to my brothers; in the presence of the congregation I will sing your praises' (2:12 quoting Psalm 22:22). Again as they gather they are told that they 'have come to Mount Zion' (12:22) and present is 'Jesus the mediator of a new covenant' (v 24). Again this focuses our thoughts on Jesus as High Priest leading the worship of God's people. When we are feeling small and feeble and that the worship we are offering is not very exciting, how this should transform and bring a sense of God's glory to what we are doing!

Where to from here? Hebrews 5:1–3 is our key text for unlocking the theme of Christ's high priesthood.

Every high priest is selected from among men and is appointed to represent them in matters related to God, to offer gifts and sacrifices for sins. He is able to help those who are ignorant and going astray, since he himself is subject to weakness. This is why he has to offer sacrifices for his own sins as well as for the sins of the people.

Our outline above summarises the teaching of the text: 'There are four essential points about High Priests—appointment by God—representing men to God and offering gifts and sacrifices and the ability, through being able to sympathise, to help the weak.'

It is these points which we will now go on to examine. As the particular focus in Hebrews is on the current priestly work of Christ in intercession we will look firstly at Christ's appointment by God as High Priest, secondly at his ability to sympathise and then at his high priestly tasks of offering and intercession.

Notes

1 **Alexander Nairne,** The Epistle of the Priesthood, p. 130.

2 **William Lane,** Word Bible Commentary Hebrews 1–8, 1991, p. cxxxviii.

3 **Peter Adam,** The Majestic Son, Anglican Information Office, 1992, p. 152.

4 **William Lane,** Word Bible Commentary Hebrews 1–8, 1991, p. cxliii.

5 **J H Thornwell,** Collected Writings volume 2, original publication 1875, Banner of Truth, 1974, p. 269.

6 **Geerhardus Vos,** Redemptive History and Biblical Interpretation, ed. R Gaffin, P&R, 1980, p. 133.

Appointment by God

A Good High Priest is come,
Supplying Aaron's place,
And taking up his room,
Dispensing life and grace,
The law by Aaron's priesthood came,
But grace and truth by Jesus' Name[1]

Why Melchizedek matters

When Spurgeon was provoked to write: 'I have a very lively, or rather a deadly, recollection of a certain series of discourses on the Hebrews, which made a deep impression on my mind of a most undesirable kind. I wished frequently that the Hebrews had kept the Epistle to themselves, for it sadly bored one poor gentile lad.'[2] I rather think it may have been the sermons on chapter 7 which finished him off. Chapter 7 deals largely with Melchizedek and his order of priesthood and so it can seem both obscure and unrelated to the needs of the reader. Certainly most people reading it are unlikely to experience a sense of instant comfort and encouragement.

The work of the High Priest as intercessor and his ability to sympathise with his tempted people is of central importance to the writer to the Hebrews and occupies most of the letter. This is the pastoral input that will enable his readers to continue faithful to Christ and, as those with a Jewish background, they will have felt quite at home with this teaching. However his first logical priority is to establish that Jesus is in fact appointed by God as High Priest. Unless his ministry is from God there is no possibility that we could benefit from it in any way and further discussion would be pointless. The fact that the writer regards appointment by God as vitally important is made clear from several verses in Hebrews 5:1–10: –

'Every high priest is selected from among men and is appointed to represent them in matters related to God'. (5:1)

'No one takes this honour upon himself; he must be called by God'. (5:4)

'[Jesus] was designated by God to be high priest in the order of Melchizedek.' (5:10)

When Jesus was announced in this way one can imagine that the readers must have wondered what on earth the writer was getting at. It was understandable to them that the writer should talk about the need for Jesus to become 'a merciful and faithful high priest in service to God, and that he might make atonement for the sins of the people. Because he himself suffered when he was tempted, he is able to help those who are being tempted' (2:17–18). They knew their need for their sins to be atoned for and knew their need of help in temptation as all believers do. It was the need to relate this to Melchizedek they found hard to understand. This is a feeling today's Christians may share. It is often shown by reluctance to devote ourselves to solid teaching and a tendency to seek a spiritual quick fix. We think: 'Why should we have to dig into the Old Testament in order to get the blessing and encouragement we need? Doesn't the Lord realize that when we feel depressed we just don't feel up to solid study? Isn't there an easier way to get help?'

This is why the writer has to put in a section to encourage and warn his readers, beginning 'We have much to say about this, but it is hard to explain because you are slow to learn' (5:11). Only after this section can he get back to his subject, 'Jesus ... has become a high priest for ever, in the order of Melchizedek' (6:20). Who was Melchizedek and why was a different type of high priest needed?

¹This Melchizedek was king of Salem and priest of God Most High. He met Abraham returning from the defeat of the kings and blessed him, ²and Abraham gave him a tenth of everything. First, his name means 'king of righteousness'; then also, 'king of Salem' means 'king of peace'. ³Without father or mother, without genealogy, without beginning of days or end of life, like the Son of God he remains a priest for ever. ⁴Just think how great he was: Even the patriarch Abraham gave him a tenth of the plunder! ⁵Now the law requires the descendants of Levi who become priests to collect a tenth

from the people—that is, their brothers—even though their brothers are descended from Abraham. [6]This man, however, did not trace his descent from Levi, yet he collected a tenth from Abraham and blessed him who had the promises. [7]And without doubt the lesser person is blessed by the greater. [8]In the one case, the tenth is collected by men who die; but in the other case, by him who is declared to be living. [9]One might even say that Levi, who collects the tenth, paid the tenth through Abraham, [10]because when Melchizedek met Abraham, Levi was still in the body of his ancestor. (Hebrews 7:1–10)

MELCHIZEDEK! WHO?

John McCarthy, who was held as a hostage by Islamic fundamentalists in Lebanon, tells the story of his own Bible reading in captivity. He was not a habitual Bible reader or committed Christian and he tells us that, 'a phrase I'd read in captivity kept coming back to me. It went something like "and in the desert there was Omar with his sheep and goats" … Re-reading the Bible, I have been unable to find this Omar'.[3] Like a lot of people who in some way have been helped by an obscure, and now dimly remembered, Old Testament passage it can be almost impossible to find again. Melchizedek is rather like the elusive Omar and only gets two mentions in the entire Old Testament, in Genesis 14 and in Psalm 110. Psalm 110:4 is the text that the teaching about Jesus as High Priest is based on: 'You are a priest for ever, in the order of Melchizedek.' Genesis 14 is the only place in the Old Testament that we get any detail about Melchizedek apart from his name and the fact of his priesthood.

In Hebrews 7:1–2 the writer summarises everything we know about Melchizedek: 'This Melchizedek was king of Salem and priest of God Most High. He met Abraham returning from the defeat of the kings and blessed him, and Abraham gave him a tenth of everything.' An important key to understanding what the writer has to say about Melchizedek in this passage is that the significant figure for the writer is not Melchizedek but Jesus. The writer is not saying that pre-Christian Jews reading about Melchizedek in Genesis 14 should see that this mysterious figure anticipates the Messiah. What he is saying is that Christians reading the Old Testament in the light of the gospel should see that this mysterious figure models a priesthood which is not Aaronic, not resting on descent from Aaron, and which can therefore provide a category for the type of priesthood that Jesus exercised.

The only reason then that Melchizedek is mentioned is to authenticate Jesus' High Priesthood. The only true priesthood in the Old Testament, barring Aaron's, belongs to Melchizedek. All other priesthoods are not priesthoods in that they do not have a relation to the true and living God. The writer shows that Jesus' is a greater High Priesthood than that of Aaron and that of all the subsequent High Priests. This is done with the aim of stopping the readers from longing for a return to the good old days that only exist in their own minds. The writer is not the type of preacher who wants to be known as a great Bible scholar, who can give all sorts of erudite, but irrelevant, Bible titbits. He does want to be an effective pastor and so all he teaches is geared to his readers and their current need of help.

MELCHIZEDEK—WHAT DO WE NEED TO KNOW ABOUT HIM?
The writer finds significance in his name and title and in what we read (and what we do not read!) about him.

His name and title. The name Melchizedek means, 'king of righteousness' (7:2), and his title, 'king of Salem' means 'king of peace' (7:2). The reason our attention is drawn to these matters is because Melchizedek is thought of as a type of Christ. By type we mean that like a prophet he points us to Christ but does so not in words but by significant facts about him and his activities. His name and title are also appropriate to Jesus the Messiah. PE Hughes writes:

In Christ we see the appearance of the expected everlasting king promised to David's line under whom righteousness flourishes and peace abounds (Psalm 72:7; cf. Psalm 97:2 and 98:3, 9): he is 'the Prince of Peace,' of the increase of whose government and peace there shall be no end (Isaiah 9:6f.); he is the long-awaited king who will speak peace to the nations (Zechariah 9:9 f.), and 'the righteous Branch,' whose name is 'The Lord our Righteousness' and who administers justice in his glorious reign (Jeremiah 23:5f; 35:15f.). As king he is just, and as priest he justifies all who trust in his atoning sacrifice (Romans 3:26; 5:8f.).[4]

The fact that he is both king and priest is remarkable in prefiguring the work of Christ. The two offices and roles were completely separated in the Old Testament arrangements. King Saul was punished by the dynastic loss of his kingdom when he usurped the task of sacrifice (1 Samuel 13:1–14). Even more dramatically, King Uzziah, who was a godly king, was immediately punished with leprosy, and hence exclusion from God's presence in worship, for the same offence (2 Chronicles 26:16–21).

What we do not read about him. We are told 'Without father or mother, without genealogy, without beginning of days or end of life, like the Son of God he remains a priest for ever' (7:3). We must note again that he is not deducing truths about Jesus from Melchizedek but noting correspondences between Jesus and Melchizedek. He does not start with Melchizedek and say, 'If Melchizedek is like this then the Messiah must be like him.' He starts with Jesus and says, 'Jesus the Messiah is like this—in what ways does Melchizedek resemble and point to him?'

One respect is that his priesthood is not established by tracing his family tree or passed on to his children. This may not amaze us but to the Jewish reader it was startling. One of the great events in the history of the Jews was the return from exile. One major task was to rebuild the temple, which of course meant that a supply of priests was needed. However because of the regulations concerning priesthood those who came forward were carefully checked and we read of some that: 'These searched for their family records, but they could not find them and so were excluded from the priesthood as unclean' (Nehemiah 7:64). Clearly another radically different type of priesthood is in view as regards Jesus.

What we do read about him. In vs 4–10 the writer then goes on to establish the point 'Just think how great he was' (v 4). This is shown by the fact that Abraham gave tithes to him (v 4) and was blessed by him (v 6). Therefore a comparison is made, 'And without doubt the lesser person is blessed by the greater' (v 7). As Levi is also included in Abraham's action (vs 9–10) the logic is that the whole body of the faithful, who live by the promises, are blessed by, and acknowledge the superiority of and their dependence on this order of priesthood that belongs to Melchizedek.

Why another kind of high priest?

We will now consider the teaching of the rest of the chapter.

[11]If perfection could have been attained through the Levitical priesthood (for on the basis of it the law was given to the people), why was there still need for another priest to come-one in the order of Melchizedek, not in the order of Aaron? [12]For when there is a change of the priesthood, there must also be a change of the law. [13]He of whom these things are said belonged to a different tribe, and no one from that tribe has ever served at the altar. [14]For it is clear that our Lord descended from Judah, and in regard to that tribe Moses said nothing about priests. [15]And what we have said is even more clear if another priest like Melchizedek appears, [16]one who has become a priest not on the basis of a regulation as to his ancestry but on the basis of the power of an indestructible life. [17]For it is declared:

> 'You are a priest for ever,
> in the order of Melchizedek.'

[18]The former regulation is set aside because it was weak and useless [19](for the law made nothing perfect), and a better hope is introduced, by which we draw near to God. [20]And it was not without an oath! Others became priests without any oath, [21]but he became a priest with an oath when God said to him:

> 'The Lord has sworn
> and will not change his mind:
> "You are a priest for ever."'

[22]Because of this oath, Jesus has become the guarantee of a better covenant. [23]Now there have been many of those priests, since death prevented them from continuing in office; [24]but because Jesus lives forever, he has a permanent priesthood. [25]Therefore he is able to save completely those who come to God through him, because he always lives to intercede for them. [26]Such a high priest meets our need—one who is holy, blameless, pure, set apart from sinners, exalted above the heavens. [27]Unlike the other high priests, he does not need to offer sacrifices day after day, first for his own sins, and then for the sins of the people. He sacrificed for their sins once for all when he offered himself. [28]For the law appoints as high priests men who are weak; but the oath, which came after the law, appointed the Son, who has been made perfect for ever. (7:11–28)

An irritating feature of my life, because it seems to occur mainly at mealtimes, is the telephone sales call. Fortunately I have an easy and polite way out of the normal sales push, which is to sell me double-glazing. We live in a new house so it is double-glazed throughout and therefore all I need to say is, 'We've got it already.' I rather imagine that a Jewish reaction to the news of a new high priest in a new order of priesthood would be, 'But we've got priests already! Why do we need another kind of high priest?' The writer gives four reasons for this:—

THE FAILURE OF THE OLD TESTAMENT LAW (VS 11–19)

As we go through the letter there will emerge a number of defects in the Old Covenant administration. However these can be summarised in one main downfall, 'for the law made nothing perfect' (v 19). The writer starts out with the premise that the priesthood has been changed. This would not have happened 'If perfection could have been attained through the Levitical priesthood' (v 11). Because priesthood and the whole order of law/covenant are inextricably interlocked this must bring with it a change in the law (v 12). This means there is no problem with the fact that 'it is clear that our Lord descended from Judah, and in regard to that tribe Moses said nothing about priests' (v 14). The basis of his appointment is God's declaration: 'You are a priest for ever, in the order of Melchizedek' (v 17 quoting Psalm 110:4). This is 'not on the basis of a regulation as to his ancestry but on the basis of the power of an indestructible life' (v 16). Bruce Demarest explains this, '[the power of an indestructible life] must be regarded as the new quality of life with which Jesus was endowed upon his exaltation to the heavenly world. ... [It] is principally descriptive of Christ as Son and High Priest in his ascended and eternal state.'5 In other words the Old Covenant priests were priests by virtue of ancestry but Jesus is high priest by virtue of ability.

The failure of the law is seen in the fact it, 'made nothing perfect' (v 19). What exactly does this mean? The words translated, 'perfect, perfection,' are used about a dozen times in Hebrews and are clearly a key to understanding the book. However the precise meaning of the expression must be worked out in each particular context. Here the law's inability is contrasted with, 'a better hope ... by which we draw near to God' (v 19). Clearly the Levitical priesthood could not ensure our access to God but Jesus has done so. The metaphor comes from the structure of the tabernacle, which is set out to demonstrate the inability of the normal worshipper to draw near to God. Firstly every Jew could enter the Courtyard of the Congregation, then only priests could enter the Priests' courtyard, and then there was the Holy Place and then the Holy of Holies or Most Holy Place. Only the High Priest could enter the Holy of Holies, the innermost sanctuary, and he could only enter on the Day of Atonement (Yom Kippur).

The superiority of appointment by an oath (vs 20–22). Some years ago my wife and I were witnesses in a court case. We had seen an incident at King's Cross Station, which ended in a member of the railway staff being charged with obstructing the police. From our viewpoint the whole incident was based on a misunderstanding and there had been no intent to obstruct. We were interviewed by the police and made statements. However once they decided to make a court case of it we had to be put on oath in order to give evidence. Nothing changed in what we said but the oath adds weight to what is said. This is exactly the point the writer makes about God's oath in Hebrews 6:16–18. JH Thornwell writes about the effect of the oath being taken on the readers of the letter: 'They would feel that the scheme could not fail; that the glory of God was so deeply concerned in its success that heaven and earth might sooner pass away than a single sinner fall short of the salvation who had fled for refuge to the hope set before him.'[6] The oath is therefore taken not to ensure God's truthfulness but for our sake and our reassurance.

Again the reasoning starts from the priesthood of Jesus and works back. Jesus' appointment is by an oath 'The Lord has sworn and will not change his mind: "You are a priest for ever"' (v 21 quoting Psalm 110:4). The Aaronic priesthood is clearly inferior because there was no oath. Jesus is the 'guarantee of a better covenant' (v 22) This is because his permanent priesthood ensures the permanency of the covenant or law under which he serves (v 12).

The superiority of a permanent priesthood (vs 23–25). When I first left college I worked for three years as a local authority social worker. It was a time of change and development in social work. The old departments dealing with children, the mentally handicapped and ill, the elderly and the physically handicapped had amalgamated. Now every social worker would have to deal with all the different types of cases. The effect of these changes and the restructuring of local government was a very rapid turnover in staff. The clients suffered because they all much preferred the old system where they knew who they were dealing with. The work suffered because there was rarely the same person dealing with the same situation for any length of time and there was no continuity of plan or approach.

Continuity has great advantages and this of course is what the Aaronic priesthood lacked. Every High Priest died and there was always a new priest there. This meant the salvation offered could not be a complete one. By contrast because Jesus 'lives for ever, he has a permanent priesthood' (v 24). There is a question as to what is the meaning of the word translated 'permanent' and it may well be intended to convey both the permanence and the non-transferability of the priesthood. The result of this is that the fact 'he always lives to intercede for them' guarantees that he can 'save completely those who come to God through him' (v 25). Again the word translated 'completely' (NIV) is ambiguous and the other possible meaning of 'for ever' (NIV margin) may well be combined with it to give the idea of 'completely and for ever.' The idea is that as we come to God through Jesus for salvation, all that we need to enable us to continue serving and worshipping God, will be given to us as we come to him and will always be given to us as we come to him.

The superiority of a sinless priesthood (vs 26–28). Here the writer clearly moves beyond Melchizedek as a type of Christ and focuses solely on Jesus himself. Christ's High Priesthood is really eternal and hence we know that he is no longer subject to death. This must mean that Christ is free from sin and death and so able to function permanently as the priest we need. In v 26 Jesus is described as 'holy, blameless, pure, set apart from sinners, exalted above the heavens.' This description shows his character, in that he is 'holy' which means, 'In mind and conduct he perfectly fulfils the divine requirements'[7] and he is also 'pure' (RSV 'unstained'), which is a word normally used for the ritual purity of things to be used in God's service but here applied to Jesus' suitability for service. Secondly the description shows his removal from his earthly scene of testing, for he is 'set apart from sinners', not referring to his moral qualities but to his exaltation to God's very presence where he is now 'exalted above the heavens.' Because of his moral purity and resulting exaltation he is different from the Aaronic high priests and 'does not need to offer sacrifices day after day, first for his own sins, and then for the sins of the people' (v 27). As regards his own sins there are none to be atoned for, and as regards the people's: 'He sacrificed for their sins once for all when he offered himself' (v 27). The 'once for all' nature of Christ's sacrifice is vital in Hebrews because, while the overall emphasis of the letter falls on Christ's present ability to help, that ability is based on the past completion of his sacrifice. The contrast is drawn in v 28 between the law appointing, and God appointing by oath 'the Son, who has been made perfect for ever.' The weakness of the Aaronic priests is their sinfulness and mortality and the son's perfection is his sinless immortality.

The main point the writer is making here is 'Such a high priest meets our need' (v 26). This refers back to 'a better hope [being] introduced by which we draw near to God' (v 19), to his solemn installation as High Priest with an oath (cf. vs 20–22), to his permanent ability to intercede (cf. v 25) and forward to his sinless character (vs 26–28). Because he is clear of either having to deal with his own sins or offer sacrifices for ours he is free and able to meet our needs for help at any time. Recently a very troubled young man we know told us that he was taking a course on counselling with a view to getting into social work of some kind. My wife and I felt immediately it was inappropriate. How could other people come to him with confidence for help with their problems when clearly he was still bogged down with his own? When drowning we look for help from someone on the shore, not a fellow struggler in the water.

Moving on

This however does not really deal with the serious problem the Hebrew Christians were facing. They accepted Jesus' greatness and ability to save, at least notionally, and doubtless it helped to know that God properly appointed him. What they needed to believe and feel was his ability to empathise with them so as to help them in temptation. This is a perennial need amongst Christians because the glorified Christ is felt to be less approachable than the Jesus of the gospel records. In the 17th Century Thomas Goodwin wrote his great treatise: 'with the aim:

To remove that great stone of stumbling ... in the thoughts of men in the way to faith, that Christ being now absent, and withal exalted to so high and infinite a distance of glory ... they cannot tell how to come to treat with him about their salvation so freely,

… as Mary, and Peter, and his other disciples did here below. … The drift of this discourse is therefore to ascertain [assure] poor souls, that his heart, in respect to pity and compassion, remains the same it was on earth.[8]

It is this subject we turn to in the next three chapters.

Notes

1 **John Cennick,** A Good High Priest is come.

2 **C H Spurgeon,** The Early Years, Banner of Truth reprint, p. 48.

3 **John McCarthy,** Transmission Spring 2000, Looking for Omar—A Bible Journey.

4 **PE Hughes,** A Commentary on the Epistle to the Hebrews, Eerdmans, 1977, pp. 247–248.

5 **Bruce Demarest,** A History of the Interpretation of Hebrews 7:1–10 from the Reformation to the Present Day, Mohr, 1976, p. 110.

6 **JH Thornwell,** Collected Writings, volume 2, original publication 1875, Banner of Truth, 1974, p. 273.

7 **F Hauck,** Theological Dictionary of the New Testament, ed. Kittel and Friedrich, Eerdmans, 1985, p. 734.

8 **Thomas Goodwin,** The Works of Thomas Goodwin, Volume 4, original publication 1651, James Nisbet and Co., 1862, p. 95.

Christ's sympathy (1)

With joy we meditate the grace
Of our High Priest above;
His heart is made of tenderness,
And overflows with love.

Touched with a sympathy within,
He knows our feeble frame;
He knows what sore temptations mean,
For he has felt the same.[1]

Why Jesus's sympathy matters

At night, just before we go to bed, my wife and I have our only period of the day when we are alone and can guarantee time to talk. Very often we go over the day's events, which often involve the stresses and strains of pastoral involvement with people. Sometimes we may need one another's advice but most often we just need someone to share what the day's events felt like. We need someone to feel with us what our lives are like and to share the experiences of our life with us. In the full meaning of the word we want sympathy. Though they needed help and direction as well, the Hebrew Christians desperately needed sympathy.

The sympathy of Jesus

One of the vital qualifications of the Lord Jesus in order to be 'a merciful and faithful high priest in service to God' (2:17), is his compassion and sympathy. In Hebrews 5:2 we are told that this is an essential qualification in any high priest: 'He is able to deal gently with those who are ignorant and are going astray, since he himself is subject to weakness.' Before we go further in our study there are two important points to note. Firstly, this is not an Old Testament emphasis. Joy Tetley writes: 'Verse 2 is, in fact, an extraordinary statement, for nowhere in the Old Testament are pastoral sympathy and gentle care presented as a feature of priesthood (cultic sacrifice, teaching and leading are, rather, the major emphases).'[2] The answer to this apparent problem is that the Aaronic priests' ability to sympathise with sinners was self-evident and could be taken for granted. After all, his weaknesses were revealed in the fact that 'he has to offer sacrifices for his own sins, as well as for the sins of the people.' (5:3). Nobody could be in any danger of feeling that any Aaronic high priest was some superhuman being who is immune to suffering and to temptation and therefore would lack understanding and sympathy.

Secondly, this emphasis is a vitally important one in writing to the Hebrews because of their failure to understand this truth about the Lord Jesus. Donald Macleod writes: 'All the indications are that the real danger in the circle addressed by the writer to the Hebrews is that they were so obsessed by the augustness of the Mediator that they tended to view him as a remote, untouchable figure, infinitely distanced from themselves.'[3] The writer addresses this problem, not by playing down Christ's deity, for he is introduced to us as 'the radiance of God's glory and the exact representation of his being,' (1:3) but by underscoring and emphasizing his identity and empathy with us. Donald Macleod writes: 'For the writer to the Hebrews, the significance of Jesus is absolute. He is Ultimate Reality. But he is Ultimate Reality in a form which is truly conversant with our human plight.'[4]

OUR NEED TO KNOW THAT JESUS CARES

The same difficulty, of feeling Christ to be remote and unapproachable, is still with us today. It is sometimes expressed in public statements about the Christian faith as well as in the pain and sense of isolation experienced by many Christians. It can be seen in the place given to Mary in some Roman Catholic devotion. In 1997 millions of signatures were collected in an appeal to the Pope to proclaim the Virgin Mary 'co-redemptrix and mediatrix of all graces'. In response to the concern expressed by both Protestants and Roman Catholics, *The Times* published an article saying that what was requested was only a refinement of doctrine. The writer went on to defend this assertion by stating: 'Precisely because she is not divine but human, Mary seems more approachable than Christ himself. If our Lord brings salvation to mankind, it is our Lady who comforts us in our troubles.'[5] It is hard to see how such a way of thinking could survive a serious reading of the letter to the Hebrews. However, unquestionably the whole cult of Mary is to be seen as a way of meeting the same felt need of Christ's seeming unapproachability due to his divinity.

Over the years I have often talked to those who have abandoned, or who are tempted to abandon, their Christian commitment. Obviously many details have varied because of the very different personal circumstances of those involved. What they do have in common is the sense that: 'It hasn't worked for me!' They feel that they have committed themselves and hoped and trusted in God only to be left feeling let down, abandoned and, most of all not understood and sympathised with. C S Lewis, writing after the death of his wife, and he was not abandoning his faith but struggling with it, captures this feeling for us:

Meanwhile, where is God? This is one of the most disquieting symptoms. When you are happy, so happy that you have no sense of needing him, so happy that you are tempted to feel his claims upon you as an interruption, if you remember yourself and turn to him with gratitude and praise, you will be—or so it seems—welcomed with open arms. But go to him when your need is desperate, when all other help is vain, and what do you find? A door slammed in your face, and a sound of bolting and double bolting on the inside. After that, silence. You may as well turn away. The longer you wait, the more emphatic the silence will become.[6]

To say that Hebrews gives us answers is not in any way to play down the reality of a sense of abandonment and pain in those who face the questions.

HOW CAN JESUS UNDERSTAND MY PROBLEMS IF HE IS GOD?

The difficulty people face in holding the biblical understanding that Jesus is truly both God and man is that they feel that his deity must in some way compromise and limit his humanity. This is a common problem in the devotion of some poorly taught evangelicals. One dear Christian lady told me that a book she had read, by a well-known evangelical author, taught that, due to his deity, Christ would not have experienced physical sufferings on the cross. The teaching aim of the book was to insist that his sufferings would have been purely spiritual. She thought that this showed great insight and was spiritually helpful. Actually, if this spiritual discovery were true, it would be a profound loss to us. It would mean that Jesus' humanity is illusory; it would certainly be very different from our humanity, and this would severely limit the comfort we might draw from his sympathy and understanding of our life and temptations. Limitations to his assumption of true humanity, that is, a humanity that is one with our humanity, are expressly denied in the classical confessions of faith. For example, the Belgic Confession, Article 18 reads, 'He truly assumed a human nature *with all its infirmities*, without sin'. However a failure to reckon on Christ's full and true humanity is a problem that lingers in the spiritual experience of countless Christians to the present day.

Jesus is fully and truly human

THE TRUE HUMANITY OF JESUS IN THE NEW TESTAMENT

We will examine the general teaching of the New Testament as a backdrop to the teaching of Hebrews with its specific pastoral application. We are faced with specific statements as well as a mass of incidental details gleaned from the gospel records.

Of the specific statements we need only take one or two, which are quite explicit. He took, 'the very nature of a servant' (Philippians 2:7). The Greek word translated: 'very nature' is *morphe* which denotes human nature with: 'both the external features by which [it] is recognised and the characteristics and qualities which are essential to it.'[7] That is saying that everything we might see which enables us to recognise a human being and everything that we know to make up our own true humanity is present in Christ. The real physical and bodily nature of the humanity of Christ can be seen in 1 John 4:2, 'Every spirit that acknowledges that Jesus Christ has come in the flesh is from God'.

The incidental details in the gospel narratives are varied and compelling in their combined weight. Just from the Gospel of Luke alone we find that Jesus is born normally (2:6–7), grows and develops both physically and spiritually (2:40, 52), is tempted by the devil and is hungry (4:2), falls asleep when tired (8:23), experiences anguish and sweats profusely (22:44) and draws attention to his resurrection body of 'flesh and bones' (24:39). Clearly it is not that there is nothing to make us say 'What kind of man is this?' (Matthew 8:27), but that there is everything to make us sing:

> Lord Jesus Christ,
> You have come to us,
> You are one with us,
> Mary's Son.[8]

The reality of Christ's humanity is also true in his possession of a true human mind and will, and also in his emotional life. Donald Macleod quotes tellingly from BB Warfield and from John Calvin in his section on Christ's 'Human Emotions':

'It belongs to the truth of our Lord's humanity', wrote BB Warfield, 'that he was subject to all sinless human emotions.' This has been strongly emphasized in Protestant theology, particularly by John Calvin. 'Christ', he wrote, 'has put on our feelings along with our flesh.' He develops this theme more fully in his exposition of Christ's agony in the garden, where, he says, Christ's mind was seized with a terror to which he had not been accustomed. This should cause us no embarrassment: 'those who imagine that the Son of God was exempt from human passions do not truly and sincerely acknowledge him to be a man.'[9]

The emotions of Jesus have not been explored often in their own right by theologians and preachers. They are most normally considered incidentally as we read through the gospel story. However BB Warfield in: *The Emotional Life of Our Lord* (quoted above) and WG Blaikie and Robert Law in *The Inner Life of Christ*[10] have attempted such studies. Warfield's is a more detailed and doctrinal study and Blaikie and Law's more devotional. They list emotions of joy, geniality, sorrow, peace, compassion (for both the suffering and the sinful), anger and amazement.

One of the most remarkable parts of Warfield's study is of Jesus' anger as expressed in his weeping at the grave of Lazarus. He writes:

Jesus, therefore, when he saw her [Mary] wailing, was enraged in spirit and troubled himself and wept. His inwardly restrained fury produced a profound agitation of his whole being, one of the manifestations of which were tears … The spectacle of the distress of Mary and her companions enraged Jesus because it brought poignantly home to his consciousness the evil of death, its unnaturalness.[11]

In other words what we have in the weeping of Jesus is not just sympathy but blazing anger and rage against the effects and cruel tyranny of sin and evil. We will consider in the next chapter the reality of temptation for Jesus and in the following chapter the reality of the emotion of fear as he experienced it. However this example of Jesus' anger makes clear that we are dealing with someone who has known the whole range of human experience and emotion. Even to the point of experiencing strong and powerful emotions which, when we experience them, almost always carry with them the taint and the abiding consciousness of our own sinfulness.

THE BOOK OF HEBREWS EMPHASIZES THE TRUE HUMANITY OF JESUS
We will examine the identification and empathy with his people shown by the Lord Jesus from the key passages in Hebrews—that is 2:5–18 (especially vs 10–18), 4:14–16 and 5:7–10. It is interesting to note that so important is this emphasis to the writer that these passages precede in Hebrews those that relate to Christ's finished work of sacrifice and continued work of intercession. This may be because those areas were clearer to the Hebrew Christians than the area of Christ's ability to sympathise. Once he had gained their confidence in Christ's ability to understand and willingness to help it only remained to underline his ability actually to provide help.

The three sections show the writer's thought about the real humanity of the Lord Jesus being developed in the perspective of the pastoral needs of his people. In 2:5–18 the thought is of the necessity of the incarnation and humble state of the Saviour in order to bring 'many sons to glory' (2:10). In 4:14–16 we move on to the reality of his human weakness and his temptations and hence his ability to sympathise and bring help to his followers. In 5:7–9 we see Jesus identified with us as authentically human in his struggle to do God's will when faced with the threat of death. In this chapter we will look at the first section, which is really introductory to the subject and places Jesus' role as High Priest in the widest possible context. 2:5–18: *Why Jesus has been made one with us.* We will first consider vs 5–9.

'It is not to angels that he has subjected the world to come, about which we are speaking. But there is a place where someone has testified:

> "What is man that you are mindful of him,
>> the son of man that you care for him?
> You made him a little lower than the angels;
>> you crowned him with glory and honour
>> and put everything under his feet."

In putting everything under him, God left nothing that is not subject to him. Yet at present we do not see everything subject to him. But we see Jesus, who was made a little lower than the angels, now crowned with glory and honour because he suffered death, so that by the grace of God he might taste death for everyone.'

In these verses the writer deals with the nature of salvation in the widest possible perspective. In the sphere of all creation, who is the noblest, greatest, and most dignified of creatures? The obvious answer would surely be the angels who were actually involved in the revelation of the law (2:2). However, though obvious, it would be the wrong answer. In 1:4–14 the exalted Son, who is fully human, is quite clearly 'superior to the angels' (1:4). More than this the general statement can be made that the angels are 'ministering spirits sent to serve those who will inherit salvation' (1:14) and so his status, as being above the angels, is shared with those he saves.

Humanity was made to rule over the creation (2:6–8 quoting Psalm 8:4–6). Currently, and very obviously, humanity has failed in this calling for (in a piece of masterly understatement), 'God left nothing that is not subject to him. Yet at present we do not see everything subject to him' (2:8). Every problem of sin, ecology, social unrest and natural disaster is summed up in this. However the answer is found in that (2:9 translated literally to bring out the emphatic word order), 'The one who was made a little lower than the angels, we see, that is Jesus'. It is Jesus who is, 'now crowned with glory and honour' (echoing Psalm 8) and who is, 'bringing many sons to glory' (2:10),—that is bringing them to share with him in the dominion over creation for which humanity was created and predestined.

We will now consider vs 10–18.

¹⁰In bringing many sons to glory, it was fitting that God, for whom and through whom everything exists, should make the author of their salvation perfect through suffering. ¹¹Both the one who makes men holy and those who are made holy are of the same family. So Jesus is not ashamed to call them brothers. ¹²He says,

> 'I will declare your name to my brothers;
> in the presence of the congregation I will sing your praises.'

¹³And again,

> 'I will put my trust in him.'

And again he says,

> 'Here am I, and the children God has given me.'

¹⁴Since the children have flesh and blood, he too shared in their humanity so that by his death he might destroy him who holds the power of death—that is, the devil—¹⁵and free those who all their lives were held in slavery by their fear of death. ¹⁶For surely it is not angels he helps, but Abraham's descendants. ¹⁷For this reason he had to be made like his brothers in every way, in order that he might become a merciful and faithful high priest in service to God, and that he might make atonement for the sins of the people. ¹⁸Because he himself suffered when he was tempted, he is able to help those who are being tempted.

These verses deal with Jesus' task of bringing many sons to glory. These sons are members of a suffering, fearful, sinful and tempted humanity (see vs 10, 15, 17–18). The reality of his incarnation is made necessary by his relatedness, as saviour, to such people. 'Both the one who makes men holy and those who are made holy are of the same family [lit. from one]' (2:11). Again 'Since the children have flesh and blood, he too shared in their humanity' (2:14). His ability to save is (v 10) made possible by his experience of suffering as he is made perfect through suffering. W L Lane writes:

The 'perfection' of Jesus in this context (cf.5:8–9, 7, 28) has functional implications. The emphasis falls on the notion that he was fully equipped for his office. God qualified Jesus to come before him in priestly action. He perfected him as a priest of his people through his sufferings, which permitted him to accomplish his redemptive mission.[12]

The teaching of the verse then is quite clearly that the task of Jesus to be a

Priest and Saviour to his people could not have been carried out without the experience of suffering in a genuinely human life. No real incarnation would mean that there is no real salvation.

Patently obviously too, his death to 'make atonement for the sins of the people' (v 17), and so that 'by his death he might destroy him who holds the power of death—that is the devil' (v 14), requires a real humanity capable of passing through death. Only one who is 'made like his brothers in every way' (v 17), could conceivably have died the death that robs Satan of all his accusing power against us, which is what makes death fearful for us. As Paul writes:

If God is for us, who can be against us? He who did not spare his own Son, but gave him up for us all—how will he not also, along with him, graciously give us all things? Who will bring any charge against those whom God has chosen? It is God who justifies. Who is he that condemns? Christ Jesus who died—more than that, who was raised to life—is at the right hand of God and is also interceding for us. (Romans 8:31–34)

It is because of the confidence we can and should have in the face of death that Calvin writes: 'an overdose of fear comes from ignorance of the grace of Christ.'[13]

The sufferings of life and death are what qualify Jesus to be 'a merciful and faithful high priest in service to God' (v 17), and 'Because he himself suffered when he was tempted, he is able to help those who are being tempted' (v 18). The idea behind the word translated 'help' is to: 'come running in a response to a cry for help',[14] which conveys something of the 'Rapid Response Force' nature of the help available.

Moving on

We shall go on in the next two chapters to look at the reality of suffering and temptation in the life of the Lord Jesus. What is important to remember at every stage in our study is that it is the same human nature that Jesus had on earth that is now glorified in heaven. Jesus having carried with his human body and nature into heaven the experience and memory of suffering and temptation, which he experienced in that same body and nature while on earth.

The hymn-writers are full of this:

He has raised our human nature
In the clouds to God's right hand;[15]

and:

O joy, there sitteth in our flesh,
Upon a throne of light,
One of a human mother born,
In perfect Godhead bright.[16]

and it is a truth that we have not perhaps, like the Hebrews, given its full place in our lives.

Notes

1 **Isaac Watts,** *With joy we meditate the grace.*

2 **Joy Tetley,** *Encounter with God in Hebrews,* Scripture Union, 1995.

3 **Donald Macleod,** *The Person of Christ,* IVP, 1998, p. 85.

4 **Donald Macleod,** *op. cit.,* p. 86.

5 **David Samuel,** 'Is Mary Co-Redeemer?', *English Churchman,* September 1997.

6 **C S Lewis,** *A Grief Observed,* Faber and Faber, 1961, p. 9.

7 **Gordon Fee,** *IVP New Testament Commentary on Philippians,* 1999, p. 93.

8 **P Appleford,** *Lord Jesus Christ you have come to us,* 1960.

9 **Donald Macleod,** *op. cit.,* p. 170.

10 Original publication by Hodder and Stoughton 1876 (1995, Tentmaker Publications).

11 **B B Warfield,** *op. cit.,* p. 116.

12 **WL Lane,** *Word Bible Commentary on Hebrews 1–8,* Word, 1991, pp. 57–58.

13 **John Calvin,** *The Epistle of Paul to the Hebrews—Epistles of Peter,* St Andrew Press, 1963, p. 31.

14 **G Abbott-Smith,** *Manual Lexicon of the New Testament,* T & T Clark, 1991, p. 83 (gleaned from comments).

15 **Christopher Wordsworth,** *See the conqueror mounts in triumph.*

16 **Edward Caswall,** *It is my sweetest comfort Lord, And will forever be, To muse upon the gracious truth, Of thy humanity.*

Christ's sympathy (2)

He once temptations knew,
Of every sort and kind,
That he might succour show
To every tempted mind:
In every point the Lamb was tried
Like us, and then for us he died.[1]

One very well known evangelical has expressed the thought that Jesus, being sinless in his humanity, would no doubt have looked very attractive, probably being a six foot tall, 180 lb hunk, and have been an outstanding natural athlete. I am not so sure about this because it seems to be contrary to two facts about Jesus' humanity that the Bible records for us. Firstly, Jesus was sent 'in the likeness of sinful man' (Romans 8: 3), and secondly 'He had no beauty or majesty to attract us to him, nothing in his appearance that we should desire him' (Isaiah 53: 2). I think that the idea has its root in the difficulty we have in accepting that Jesus really is like us in our own humanity—we feel that somehow his experience of being human ought to be more trouble free than our own. This difficulty is relevant as we move on from looking at the reality of, and the reasons for, Christ's incarnation in full humanity to look at the reality of his temptation and suffering which enables him to help us.

He once temptations knew,
Of every sort and kind,
That he might succour show
To every tempted mind.

One of our problems in looking at Christ's sympathy is that we can more easily conceive of it being directed to us as suffering than being directed to us as being tempted to sin. The result of this is that while we might think it legitimate to draw comfort from Jesus' sympathy when we suffer, we hesitate to draw the same comfort when we are tempted to sin. It seems to belittle Jesus' sinlessness to say that he fully understands our temptations to sin. But John Cennick was quite right in his interpretation of scripture in the above hymn. Jesus not only knows the reality of suffering but also the reality of temptation to sin that often accompanies suffering. As we look at our passages, Hebrews 4:14–16 and Hebrews 5:7–10, we will have in mind these two aspects of his sympathy. Hebrews 4:14–16, which we will focus on in this chapter, states the general principle about Jesus' sympathy with sinners. In the next chapter we will examine Hebrews 5:7–10 which deals with a specific incident in his life and applies the experience to his ongoing calling to be a High Priest for us.

Therefore, since we have a great high priest who has gone through the heavens, Jesus the Son of God, let us hold firmly to the faith we profess. For we do not have a high priest who is unable to sympathise with our weaknesses, but we have one who has been tempted in every way, just as we are yet was without sin. Let us then approach the throne of grace with confidence, so that we may receive mercy and grace to help us in our time of need (Hebrews 4:14–16).

The imperatives—which are to 'hold firmly to the faith we profess' and to 'approach the throne of grace with confidence, so that we may receive mercy and grace to help us in our time of need' are based firmly on the indicative statements about Christ's enthroned but sympathetic priesthood. As we are to regard Hebrews as a sermon the following quotation from David Jackman is appropriate: 'Biblical preaching must reflect biblical patterns, by which I mean there should be no imperatives without the indicatives, no commands without promises, no challenges without the divine resources being revealed.'[2] The writer is always concerned to get this balance right and always draws our attention to the truth of Christ's priesthood before moving to exhortations and instructions based on it.

The background to these verses

The writer has been teaching his readers some basic lessons about the life of faith. He has compared those who experienced the Old Testament salvation of deliverance from Egypt and a journey to the promised rest of Canaan with his hearers (see 3:7–4:11). There are points in common and in contrast. Both groups have heard the gospel of deliverance (4:2). Both groups have had God's rest held out to them in the promise of the gospel they have heard (4:3–11). However, despite its appeal as a source of epic films and cartoons, the story of the Exodus ultimately ends in failure for everyone except Joshua and Caleb. The Israelites whom Moses led out of Egypt failed to enter the promised land through lack of faith (4:2) and resulting disobedience (4:6). In contrast, the Hebrew Christians are encouraged to perseverance (3:14) and to vigorous, obedient faith (4:11) in order to enter the rest of God's eternal Sabbath (4:9). One very important spiritual lesson we are meant to learn is to balance the biblical teaching about perseverance as a grace given with the biblical teaching about perseverance as a duty to be performed by us. It is perseverance as a duty and as a sign of grace (3:14) with which the writer is mainly concerned.

If any warning about overconfidence needed sounding there is a loud alarm bell ringing in 4:12–13, which immediately precede our text. God's word, and the reference must be back to the gospel promise heard by his people, is 'living and active' and disobedience is no light matter. A Chinese girl who we knew once told my wife how she was evangelised. In God's goodness it was effective but not because of its Biblical correctness! The girls witnessing to her said: 'Look, put your trust in Jesus and if you don't like it you can always give it up.' God used their zeal to bring about her conversion, but their way of expressing the gospel was wrong. Coming to faith in Jesus is not a simple matter of 'take it or leave it', which is an attitude which might be quite acceptable if we were considering adopting a philosophy of life or a political creed. Wrongly handled, God's word is a dangerous weapon and its use and abuse actually reveal, 'the thoughts and attitudes of the heart' (4:12–13). God's word and our reactions to it, either of belief or unbelief, make public God's secret knowledge of the state of our heart.

What the writer wants the Hebrews to do

They are to 'hold firmly to the faith we profess' (v 14). That is to their faith in Jesus as Lord and Saviour and Son of God, together with a life that reflects that faith. The writer to the Hebrews would be totally dismissive of those who abandon an open Christian commitment that involves meeting regularly with other Christians and an obedient Christian lifestyle but claim, 'I still believe in my heart.'

It is noticeable that very often the writer will say, 'let us' rather than, 'you must'. In pastoral relationships, and preachers do well to remember this, there is great wisdom in identifying with those whom we are teaching and leading. Much resentment may be removed if those being taught realize their teacher is teaching and encouraging as a fellow-walker in the journey of faith and not shouting advice from the comfort of a spiritual limousine.

They are to 'approach the throne of grace with confidence'—the force of this is to 'again and again draw near to the throne of grace'[3] As Calvin expresses it, 'the throne is not marked by a naked majesty which overpowers us, but is adorned with a new name, that of grace.'[4] Throughout our lives we are to approach God, from whom grace flows to the people of God, in prayer. Under the Old Covenant this privilege of drawing near was restricted to the High Priest. William Lane comments: 'In a bold extension of the language of worship the writer calls the community to recognise that through the high priestly ministry Christ has achieved for them what Israel never enjoyed, namely immediate access to God and the freedom to draw near to him continually.'[3] PE Hughes writes: 'This was dramatically symbolised by the rending of the temple curtain from top to bottom at the time of the crucifixion, indicating that through an act of divine grace access into the holiest was now available to all the people.'[5]

The confidence involved is the knowledge of both a right to speak and a right to speak frankly. The original use of the Greek word was for the rights of the citizens of the Greek cities to speak in their public gatherings. A fitting illustration is the system of church organisation we have at the Congregational Church of which I am pastor. Our members' meeting is central to our church life. At these meetings, the humblest member speaks by right and they can have confidence that everyone else recognises their right to do so. However nobody else may speak to the meeting without a special invitation from the church. Later writers saw this concept of confidence as a vivid expression of a right attitude in prayer.

This means we must never put on a good face with God or feel we should not bare our hearts to him or trouble him with our needs. John Calvin encourages us to see Christ's willingness to help: 'if we were so persuaded that Christ were holding his hand out to us, who would not seize the full boldness of approaching?'[6] God knows our hearts and needs and worries and invites us to approach him for 'mercy' and 'grace' and 'timely help'. There is a contrast in tenses here—we are to continually approach but the supply of help is in response to the needs of the moment. God does not give off-the-peg help but it is always tailor-made for our particular need.

What the writer wants the Hebrews to realize

Jesus has 'gone through the heavens'—the tense used indicates that this going through the heavens to God's immediate presence means that he is now permanently to be found there. The putting together of the name 'Jesus' and the title 'Son of God', suggest that we are to bear in mind Christ's two natures and to have 'the assurance of sympathy and power.'[7] As we have come to see the problems and misunderstandings that weakened the faith of the Hebrew Christians, it is the sympathy about which they need to be convinced and it is to this that the writer now directs us.

The double negative, 'do not have … who is unable' is a literary device to make a very forceful statement: 'we *do have* … who *is able*'. To sympathise means literally 'to suffer with' and indicates that Jesus does more than feel sorry for us. In the English language the idea of sympathy has weakened into 'feels sorry for' and we have introduced another word, empathy, to take up the idea of actually experiencing something with somebody. Jesus actually shares with us in the experience of weakness and temptation and pressure. Isaac Watts expressed this well and tells us that Jesus:

And, though exalted, feels afresh
What every member bears.[8]

In addition sympathy 'always includes the element of active help.'[9] Christ's sympathy is not his sentiment about us but his identifying with us, and his commitment to us. Michael Bruce brilliantly sums up this teaching on Christ's sympathy:

In every pang that rends the heart,
The Man of Sorrows had a part;
He sympathises with our grief,
And to the sufferer sends relief[10]

Jesus fully sympathises with us in temptation

The question still remains as to what it is in our situation the Son of God actually sympathises with. We looked in the last chapter at the reality of his incarnation. He became a real human being and experienced the weakness, frailty and dependence inherent in genuine humanity. This in turn led to the suffering, which is part of our human life in a fallen world. Though it is a good start when we get to grips with the reality of Christ's humanity there is still a further step to take in our understanding.

This step is to realize that Jesus has experienced in full the experience of temptation to sin known by us. The expression used to describe this experience is again very forceful and involves a doubling up of statements to underline it: 'in every respect, in quite the same way as we are.'[11] As with us, the experience of testing, which is made possible by our ignorance and weakness, is turned into temptation to sin by the devil. We see this in the temptations in the desert (Matthew 4:1–11) and in the cry 'Come down from the cross, if you are the Son of God' (Matthew 27:40). It is important for us to see how this mirrors our own temptations, for there is a tendency to see temptation wrongly. We tend to think of sin only in terms of specific acts, like the so-called seven deadly sins, instead of as rebellion against God's will. We are God's children and his promise assures us of his love. Our temptation is to doubt that love and to desert our calling because we have been fooled into believing that happiness and success are to be found outside God's will. Jesus' temptation was to depart from the path to glory the Father had for him. We view this in the desert, when he is tempted to supply his own needs and take a short cut to glory; in the garden, when he is tempted to follow his own will not the Father's; and on the cross, when he is tempted to cut short his suffering. Ultimately this is exactly the same temptation the Hebrew Christians were going through in their temptation to desert the gospel.

The objection that because Jesus experienced temptations 'without sin', he cannot really identify with us in our experience of temptation is groundless. The reservation that the temptation is without sin does not apply to the experience of testing but to its outcome. So 'the sinlessness of Jesus does not consist in the absence of human weakness, but in an ever-renewed victory over temptations.'[12] The point is rightly made that our failure in this matter desensitises us to the forcefulness of temptation. Keith Weston illustrated this very vividly in a sermon at the Keswick Convention. He asked his hearers to imagine a man who can neither die nor lose consciousness being subject to a frenzied knife attack. At the point where, mercifully, we would pass out and experience no more pain this man will still experience in full every thrust of the knife and every iota of pain and suffering being inflicted. By analogy he suggests that our sinfulness and frequent surrender to temptation actually prevents us fully appreciating the strength and pain of temptation and that Christ's sinlessness is what enables this full understanding.

Jesus' real experience of temptation is not just of historic or theological interest. The perfect tense of the word translated 'tempted' indicates that Jesus has taken into heaven with him the experience of this temptation. This means that when we come to him we come to him as one entirely able to identify with and help us in our temptations. We also come to him as one who is deeply and passionately concerned with our situation. His presence in heaven is not to be interpreted as implying a detachment from our hurts and needs. Concerning this Andrew Bonar writes: 'Christ's heart was left here when his body went up yonder.'[13]

Moving on

Clearly the climax of Christ's temptations and testing came in the Garden of Gethsemane as the cross approached for him. It is to examine the way in which the writer to the Hebrews sees these events that we now proceed.

Notes

1 **John Cennick,** *A good High Priest is come.*
2 **David Jackman,** *Ten Growing Churches,* ed. Eddie Gibbs, Marc Europe, 1984, pp. 86–87.
3 **William Lane,** *Word Bible Commentary on Hebrews 1–8,* p. 115.

4 **John Calvin,** *The Epistle of Paul to the Hebrews and the Epistles of Peter,* St Andrews Press, 1963, p. 57.

5 **PE Hughes,** *A Commentary on the Epistle to the Hebrews,* Eerdmans, 1977, p. 173.

6 **John Calvin,** *op. cit.,* pp. 56–57.

7 **BF Westcott** in **PE Hughes,** *op. cit.,* p. 170.

8 **Isaac Watts,** *With joy we meditate the grace—Of our High Priest above.*

9 **William Lane,** *op. cit.,* p. 114.

10 **Michael Bruce,** *Where high the heavenly temple stands.*

11 **William Lane,** *op. cit.,* p. 114.

12 **Hering** in **PE Hughes,** *op. cit.,* p. 173.

13 **Andrew Bonar,** *Heavenly Springs,* original publication 1904, Banner of Truth, 1986, p. 183.

Christ's sympathy (3)

Go to dark Gethsemane,
Ye that feel the tempter's power;
Your Redeemer's conflict see;
Watch with Him one bitter hour;
Turn not from his griefs away;
Learn of Jesus Christ to pray.[1]

Jesus went out as usual to the Mount of Olives, and his disciples followed him. On reaching the place, he said to them, 'Pray that you will not fall into temptation.' He withdrew about a stone's throw beyond them, knelt down and prayed, 'Father, if you are willing, take this cup from me; yet not my will, but yours be done.' An angel from heaven appeared to him and strengthened him. And being in anguish, he prayed more earnestly, and his sweat was like drops of blood falling to the ground.

When he rose from prayer and went back to the disciples, he found them asleep, exhausted from sorrow. 'Why are you sleeping?' he asked them. 'Get up and pray so that you will not fall into temptation.' (Luke 22:39–46)

Jesus' climactic experience of temptation

J C Ryle comments on the scene in Gethsemane: 'Would we know something of the unspeakable love of Christ? Would we comprehend Christ's ability to sympathise with those in trouble? Then let the agony of the garden come often into our minds. The depth of that agony may give us some idea of our debt to Christ.'[2] It is precisely this that the writer to the Hebrews is doing as he focuses our thoughts on Jesus' experience and prayer in the garden.

Here we return to the section in Hebrews where the writer lays down the qualifications for high priesthood. It is very noticeable that his first priority, after cursorily touching on the appointment of Jesus as a High Priest according to the order of Melchizedek, is to establish the fact that 'He is able to deal gently with those who are ignorant and are going astray' (Hebrews 5:2). The way he does this is to establish that Jesus went through an experience, when facing the reality of the cross, that would enable him to identify with and help the Hebrew Christians in their own fear of suffering and death. In this respect the teaching of Hebrews on Christ's ability to sympathise will here reach its climax.

7During the days of Jesus' life on earth, he offered up prayers and petitions with loud cries and tears to the one who could save him from death, and he was heard because of his reverent submission. 8Although he was a son, he learned obedience from what he suffered 9and, once made perfect, he became the source of eternal salvation for all who obey him 10and was designated by God to be high priest in the order of Melchizedek (Hebrews 5:7–10).

We will consider first the reality of the experience of temptation in v 7. Then secondly the experience of learning obedience and being 'made perfect', and so appointed as our great High Priest, as described in vs 8–10.

The experience of temptation

This is defined for us as taking place (literally) 'During the days of his flesh', which points to his passage through his life on earth in which he fully knew the weakness and dependency involved in being genuinely human. The aorist tenses in the rest of the passage indicate a particular event or short period of time is in view, which is clearly the time Jesus spent in the Garden of Gethsemane immediately prior to his arrest. PE Hughes writes: 'The occasion intended here is beyond doubt Christ's agony in the Garden of Gethsemane, where, face to face with the awful reality of the cross, he sensed the overwhelming horror of the ordeal that lay before him and besought the Father that, if possible, this cup might be removed from him.'3

While unquestionably the Garden of Gethsemane provides the setting for the, 'prayers and petitions with loud cries and tears', it is reasonable to argue that the 'reverent submission' characterised his whole passion rather than specifically his words in prayer. His silence in the judgement hall, as well as the acquiescence with his Father's will in the garden, are eloquent evidence of his bowing to his Father's will in all the horror and terror it clearly brought to him.

Jesus' fear

In seeking to understand the temptation faced by Jesus we need to see what it was that caused him to fear, and his real desire to escape from the experience which lay before him. His fear is caused by 'this cup' (Matthew 26:39), which is clearly the forthcoming experience of betrayal and crucifixion. None of us will be fully confronted by the reality of our own death until it comes, although experiences of depressive illness, or a near miss physical escape from death, can impress the reality of our own mortality upon us. So Jesus saying, 'My soul is overwhelmed with sorrow to the point of death' (Matthew 26:38), credibly reflects the onrushing reality of his death as it overwhelms his human consciousness. Having suffered a period of serious depression this is something that I can identify with in a limited way. In my experience of depression, my own death, which is obviously a permanent part of my background consciousness, became such an overwhelming reality that I used to wake up at night completely gripped by a terror of dying.

However, to speak of Jesus' experience as being an experience purely on the level of other men and women facing or anticipating death is surely inadequate. For a start many martyrs, religious and otherwise, have faced death with greater calmness and resolution. Rather as Hugh Martin expresses it:

His sorrow arose from the source that his prayer was concerned with—the vivid view and near approach of that cup which the father was just giving him to drink. That curse of God, from which he came to redeem his elect people—that sword of the Lord's wrath and vengeance which he had just predicted—the penal desertion of the cross— the withdrawal of all comfortable [comforting] views and influences—and the present consciousness of the anger of God against him as surety-substitute, a person laden with iniquity—these were the elements mingled in the cup of trembling which was now to be put into his hands.[4]

The fear of death he experiences is inseparably connected with the particular death he must die as Saviour and Redeemer. Joseph Hart makes exactly the same point devotionally:

> Great High Priest, we view thee stooping
> With our names upon Thy breast,
> In the garden groaning, drooping,
> To the ground with horrors pressed;
>
> Holy angels stood confounded,
> To behold their maker thus;
> And can we remain unmoved,
> When we know it was for us?

Jesus' prayer

What then is involved in his prayer 'My Father, if it is possible, may this cup be taken from me'? (Matthew 26:39) Calvin uses his exposition of these words to confront an ancient heresy but in doing so captures the essence of the temptation: 'This passage clearly shows how unintelligent were the old heretics called "Monothelites", who made Christ to be endowed with only one simple will, holding that as far as he was God, he only willed the Father's Will. It follows then that his human soul had different desires from the hidden purpose of God.'[5]

Judging from a recent article I was given to read, which claimed to solve the problem of Jesus appearing to have a will different from that of his father, the heresy is by no means dead. People find it hard to accept the teaching that Jesus had a will not in line with his Father's in every respect. The reality of that differing will is actually the entire point of citing the experience as an experience of temptation. Without acknowledging the existence of a human will that genuinely revolted from the idea of such a death, the idea of Christ's real temptability is meaningless. The loss that such a failure to understand Christ's sufferings would bring is immense. Calvin, commenting on the words 'began to be sorrowful' (Matthew 26:37), writes: 'if we are ashamed of his fear and sorrow, our redemption will trickle away and be lost.'[6]

The strength of Jesus' revulsion from the experience of death facing him is plain. For 'he offered up prayers and petitions with loud cries and tears to the one who could save him from death' and in his intense, threefold repetition of his prayer he was 'in anguish … and his sweat was like drops of blood falling to the ground' (Luke 22:44). For Jesus the death of the cross is unfaceable but disobedience to the Father is unthinkable. It is from this tension that his agony stems.

It is only as 'An angel from heaven appeared to him and strengthened him' (Luke 22:43), that Jesus is enabled to continue with his prayer for 'not my will, but yours be done' (v 42). His frail humanity needs the strengthening influences of one of the 'ministering spirits sent to serve those who inherit salvation' (Hebrews 1:14) and thus he is squarely placed with us as being human and dependent. In his, 'reverent submission' he chooses his Father's will against the genuine attraction of the alternative course of action. The word translated, 'reverent submission' is very rare in the New Testament but carries with it the idea of being 'devout' or 'pious' when this is motivated by 'awe' or 'fear of God.' The thought then is that Jesus' obedience is motivated by his right attitude to God and that this attitude leads to his prayers being answered.

Was Jesus' prayer really answered?

We do need to ask how it is that Jesus' prayers are said to have been answered for it is hardly clear to us that they are. We read that, 'he offered up prayers and petitions with loud cries and tears to the one who could save him from death, and he was heard because of his reverent submission', which certainly suggests a positive outcome. However the events that follow show that Jesus did have to accept his Father's will and that included death on the cross. In what sense then can we say that, 'he was heard' and that his prayer was answered? Calvin sums it up well:

In what way was Christ heard out of his fear, when He underwent the death which he shrank from? My answer is that we must look to the point of his fear. Why did he dread death except that He saw in it the curse of God, and that He had to wrestle with the total sum of human guilt and with the powers of darkness themselves? Hence his fear and anxiety, because the judgement of God is more than terrifying. He got what He wanted inasmuch as He emerged from the pains of death as Conqueror, was upheld by the saving hand of the Father, and after a brief encounter gained a glorious victory over Satan, sin and the powers of hell.7

It is not a cop-out to say that his prayer is answered in that he retained faith in God through death and then obtained victory over it.

Jesus' experience of learning obedience and being made perfect

Again we are faced with the use of expressions about Jesus' experience which at first sight could cause problems. Was Jesus not obedient before he 'learned obedience'? Was he not perfect before being 'made perfect'? The surprise is not something that just exists because we have somehow misunderstood what is being said. The writer acknowledges the surprise element here by saying, 'Although he was a son, he learned obedience from what he suffered' and clearly shows that he is stretching the understanding of the Hebrew Christians. They have truly grasped that Jesus is 'The Son' (1:3) and now they have to take on board the reality that, in some sense at least, only through suffering has he learned obedience and been made perfect.

HOW JESUS LEARNED OBEDIENCE FROM SUFFERING

Clearly in saying, 'Although he was a son' the writer is assuming the readers' agreement that Jesus is uniquely God's Son. From the way in which the letter begins, with Jesus being described as 'the radiance of God's glory and the exact representation of his being' (1:3), his identity as one in essence with the Father is not for a moment in doubt. The key area that the writer wants to inform his readers of is the fact that Jesus had actually learned obedience and developed in his experience as a result of sufferings. Christians know that their own discipleship and obedience has been honed and developed through the experience of suffering. They need to grasp that Jesus' humanity is so closely parallel to theirs that the same can be said of him.

The fact that Christians learn through suffering is a New Testament commonplace, as Romans 5:3 makes clear, 'we also rejoice in our sufferings, because we know that suffering produces perseverance, perseverance, character; and character, hope.' James 1:2–4 and 1 Peter 1:6–7 teach the same truths in very similar words. What perhaps we fail to see or emphasise as we should is that the learning is not an automatic result of suffering, but takes place through obedience to God's will in new situations of testing. DM Lloyd-Jones writes (about experiencing testing through chastisement):

The only people who are going to derive benefit … are those who submit to God's treatment. If you shake it off, the treatment will do you no good; if you faint under it, it will do you no good; if you become bitter, it will do you no good. It only does you good if you submit to the process.[8]

In the same sense, yet without the failure that mars our life experience, the life of Jesus is one of cumulative and developing obedience to his Father. His incarnation is an act of obedience; 'I have come to do your will, O God' (Hebrews 10:7 quoting Psalm 40:8). So is his life; 'I seek not to please myself but him who sent me' (John 5:30) and so is his death; 'he humbled himself and became obedient to death—even death on a cross' (Philippians 2: 8). So much is this so that Jesus is pattern, enabler and inspiration for our own obedience; 'Let us fix our eyes on Jesus, the author and perfecter of our faith, who for the joy set before him endured the cross, scorning its shame, and sat down at the right hand of God' (Hebrews 12:2).

WHAT IT MEANT FOR JESUS TO BE MADE PERFECT
The result of these sufferings is that he was 'once made perfect' and so became 'the source of eternal salvation for all who obey him' by being 'designated by God to be a high priest in the order of Melchizedek.' Here the perfection is clearly not merely moral but vocational—that is, moral with a view to his priesthood. In other words Jesus is equipped for his calling as a High Priest by his experiences of suffering and the obedience learnt in this crucible of temptation. So though at all stages of his life Jesus is morally perfect, yet he is not perfect as regards his calling until he has passed through his life and death experiences of suffering. David Peterson writes: 'His human experience is presented as a preparation for his once-for-all act of atonement and the extension of his work into eternity.'[9]

Jesus' future work of heavenly intercession is going to involve the supplying of mercy and appropriate gracious help to all his people. Some of them may experience situations of intense suffering and be tempted to abandon their calling and obedience. Currently Christians in the Sudan, Indonesia and Iran live with the risk of martyrdom a conscious reality. An Iranian Muslim told me, concerning another Iranian who had converted from Islam to Christianity, 'In our country his life is free'—meaning that any Muslim could kill him at will and could do so without endangering his own freedom. It is hard for us in the West to imagine the pressures to give in and abandon the Christian faith that many of our brothers and sisters know all too well.

Jesus, in order to be an effective and sympathetic High Priest needs both to understand his people's temptations and to be able to help them appropriately. What is now true about Jesus, as was not true before, is that he has taken into heaven, as a necessary qualification for his ongoing work, his human experiences of suffering and temptation. And, equally importantly, he has taken into heaven his experience of God's grace and faithful help, which has enabled him to continue faithful in this intense crucible of temptation.

Isaac Watts captures well what this means for us:

With joy we meditate the grace
Of our High Priest above;
His heart is made of tenderness
And overflows with love.

Touched with a sympathy within,
He knows our feeble frame;
He knows what sore temptations mean,
For he has felt the same.

But spotless, innocent and pure,
The great Redeemer stood,
While Satan's fiery darts he bore,
And did resist to blood.

He in the days of feeble flesh
Poured out his cries and tears;
And though exalted, feels afresh
What every member bears.

Chapter 6

He'll never quench the smoking flax,
But raise it to a flame;
The bruised reed he never breaks,
Nor scorns the meanest name.

Then let our humble faith address
His mercy and his power:
We shall obtain delivering grace
In the distressing hour.

Summing up

It is important that in presenting Jesus as our great and sympathetic high priest we do not portray the Father as august, remote and legalistic and as being reluctantly persuaded to sympathise with us. The Father sends the Son as the expression of his love and concern. The Son reveals to us the Father 'When [a man] looks at me, he sees the one who sent me' (John 12:45). Regarding his own sympathy and experience he is saying in fact that: 'in the most literal sense, "God knows". God knows the truth of our condition, and not just from a holy distance. God has inside knowledge.'[10]

Notes

1 **James Montgomery,** *Go to dark Gethsemane, Ye that feel the tempter's power.*

2 **J C Ryle,** *Expository Thoughts on Luke,* volume 2, p. 423.

3 **PE Hughes,** *Commentary on Hebrews,* Eerdmans, 1977, p. 182.

4 **Hugh Martin,** *The Shadow of Calvary,* first publication 1875, Banner of Truth, 1983, p. 19.

5 **John Calvin,** *A Harmony of the Gospels,* volume III, St Andrews Press, 1972, p. 151.

6 **John Calvin,** *op. cit.,* p. 147.

7 **John Calvin,** *The Epistle of Paul to the Hebrews/The Epistles of Peter,* St Andrews Press, 1972, p. 65.

8 **DM Lloyd-Jones,** *Spiritual Depression,* Pickering and Inglis, 1965, p. 254.

9 **David Peterson,** *Hebrews and Perfection,* SNTSMS 4, 1982, chapter 4.

10 **Joy Tetley,** *Encounter with God in Hebrews,* Scripture Union, 1995, p. 64.

Christ's work of sacrifice

Jesus, my great High Priest,
Offered his blood and died;
My guilty conscience seeks
No sacrifice beside;
His powerful blood did once atone,
And now it pleads before the throne.[1]

To prepare for reading this chapter you will find it helpful to read from Hebrews 8:1 to 10:18. Though most of the text is quoted in this chapter, the themes it deals with are interwoven throughout the whole passage and so its full impact and teaching can only really be appreciated by reading the passage through in a single sitting.

The cross of Jesus and his intercession
When he was being interviewed for church membership, DL Moody was asked the question, 'What has Jesus done for you?' He replied that he was sure that Jesus had done a great deal for him but that he couldn't bring anything particular to mind. Understandably his application for membership was deferred until he could bring a more satisfactory answer. The apostle Paul wrote to the Corinthians, 'For I resolved to know nothing while I was with you except Jesus Christ and him crucified' (1 Corinthians 2: 2) and he said this because the cross is absolutely central to the good news about Jesus. We would expect that any Christian who was asked what Jesus had done for them would be able to answer and say that Jesus had died on the cross for the sins of his people. The question we are to examine in this chapter is how Jesus' death on the cross relates to his present intercession for us. It is important that we examine this because the intercession of Jesus, rather than the cross of Jesus, is the focus of the help that the writer to the Hebrews brings to his readers.

From Hebrews 5:1, 'to represent [men] in matters related to God, to offer gifts and sacrifices for sins' we have already seen that offering sacrifice and intercession are the two aspects of Jesus' priestly work. Traditionally the offering of sacrifice is spoken of as his finished work 'After he had provided purification for sins he sat down at the right hand of the Majesty in heaven' (1:3) This emphasis contrasts with the ongoing work of intercession performed by Jesus; 'he always lives to intercede for them' (7:25). While the current work of intercession is the particular emphasis that the writer majors on in his pastoral treatment of the Hebrew Christians' needs, the finished work of sacrifice is, like Jesus' appointment by God, one of the vital foundations for the intercession. In this chapter we will examine his finished sacrificial work and in the next three chapters his present work of intercession.

The teaching methods used in Hebrews

Like all good teachers, the writer's method is to move from things his readers are clear about to what they do not yet understand. Jesus in his parables goes from the well-known facts of village and farm life, a friend who has a guest arrive in the middle of the night and enemies sowing bad seed on your land, to the secrets of his kingdom. Our writer moves from the Levitical priesthood and its sacrifices, which his readers had grown up with and took for granted, to Jesus' ministry as our great High Priest. Therefore his argument is expressed in terms of old covenant practices and places. To fully appreciate the teaching of the writer to the Hebrews on Christ's sacrifice we will need to consider:—

1 The covenant arrangements under which Jesus makes his offering.
2 The sanctuary where Jesus presents his offering.
3 The accomplishment of Christ's sacrifice.

What the writer does is to set up a series of contrasts, which reveal how much better Jesus' accomplishment is than the old covenant sacrifices and offerings. The reason he deals with the subject in this way is to dissuade them from giving up on their Christian faith by returning to the Jewish community and faith.

The covenant and Jesus's sacrifice

6But the ministry Jesus has received is as superior to theirs as the covenant of which he is mediator is superior to the old one, and it is founded on better promises. 7For if there had been nothing wrong with that first covenant, no place would have been sought for another. 8But God found fault with the people and said:

> 'The time is coming, declares the Lord,
> when I will make a new covenant
> with the house of Israel
> and with the house of Judah.
> 9It will not be like the covenant
> I made with their forefathers
> when I took them by the hand
> to lead them out of Egypt,
> because they did not remain faithful to my covenant,
> and I turned away from them, declares the Lord.
> 10This is the covenant I will make with the house of Israel
> after that time, declares the Lord.
> *I will put my laws in their minds*
> and write them on their hearts.
> I will be their God,
> and they will be my people.
> 11No longer will a man teach his neighbour,
> or a man his brother, saying, 'Know the Lord,'
> because they will all know me,
> from the least of them to the greatest.
> 12For I will forgive their wickedness
> and will remember their sins no more.'

13By calling this covenant 'new,' he has made the first one obsolete; and what is obsolete and ageing will soon disappear (Hebrews 8:6–13).

Planned obsolescence, such as that referred to in v 13, is normally an irritant, rather than a cause for thankfulness. For many years our family had an electric cooker, which from time to time needed minor repairs. We eventually got to the stage where only one shop could get hold of the parts for it. Finally even they had to admit defeat and we, not without a few grumbles, had to buy a new cooker. We had been defeated by planned obsolescence. Our grumble was that the cooker could still have been made to work and the change meant extra expense. However, as far as the writer is concerned, the old covenant had never worked properly and is replaced free of charge by something far better.

According to 7:11, 'perfection' was not attainable through the Levitical priesthood on which the law or old covenant was based. The law was clearly not based on the priesthood in the sense that the priesthood came first in time. In fact the priesthood was set up under the arrangements made in the law. The meaning is that the law could not function without the priesthood and so any change in the priesthood spelt an inevitable change in the law (7:12). The need for a new covenant is confirmed in chapter 8:8–12 where the new covenant promise of Jeremiah 31:31–34 is quoted. In 8:13 we are told this makes the old covenant 'obsolete', which is a very strong term and in the Septuagint, 'denotes the uselessness of worn out things.'[2] One of the answers then to the question, 'Why do we need another high priest?' is that the old one, and the covenant under which he serves, is obsolete and useless.

The sanctuary where Jesus presents his offering

The point of what we are saying is this: We do have such a high priest, who sat down at the right hand of the throne of the Majesty in heaven, and who serves in the sanctuary, the true tabernacle set up by the Lord, not by man.(Hebrews 8:1–2)

If he were on earth, he would not be a priest, for there are already men who offer the gifts prescribed by the law. They serve at a sanctuary that is a copy and shadow of what is in heaven. This is why Moses was warned when he was about to build the tabernacle: 'See to it that you make everything according to the pattern shown you on the mountain.'(Hebrews 8:4–5)

[1]Now the first covenant had regulations for worship and also an earthly sanctuary. [2]A tabernacle was set up. In its first room were the lampstand, the table and the consecrated bread; this was called the Holy Place, [3]Behind the second curtain was a room called the Most Holy Place [4]which had the golden altar of incense and the gold-covered ark of the covenant. This ark contained the gold jar of manna, Aaron's staff that had budded, and the stone tablets of the covenant. [5]Above the ark were the

cherubim of the Glory, overshadowing the atonement cover. But we cannot discuss these things in detail now.

[6]When everything had been arranged like this, the priests entered regularly into the outer room to carry on their ministry. [7]But only the high priest entered the inner room, and that only once a year, and never without blood, which he offered for himself and for the sins the people had committed in ignorance. [8]The Holy Spirit was showing by this that the way into the Most Holy Place had not yet been disclosed as long as the first tabernacle was still standing. [9]This is an illustration for the present time, indicating that the gifts and sacrifices being offered were not able to clear the conscience of the worshipper. [10]They are only a matter of food and drink and various ceremonial washings—external regulations applying until the time of the new order.

[11]When Christ came as high priest of the good things that are already here, he went through the greater and more perfect tabernacle that is not man-made, that is to say, not a part of this creation [12]He did not enter by means of the blood of goats and calves; but he entered the Most Holy Place once for all by his own blood, having obtained eternal redemption. (Hebrews 9:1–12)

[23]It was necessary, then, for the copies of the heavenly things to be purified with these sacrifices, but the heavenly things themselves with better sacrifices than these. [24]For Christ did not enter a man-made sanctuary that was only a copy of the true one; he entered heaven itself, now to appear for us in God's presence. (Hebrews 9:23–24)

On my shelves I have a number of books which explore the spiritual significance of the design and ritual arrangements of the tabernacle. Almost invariably they are more imaginative than convincing in their explanations and some of the devotional use they make of particular details leave me thinking, 'How do they know it means that?' When, in chapter 9:1–10 we have spelt out the significance of the 'earthly sanctuary' (v 1) the authors of these books might have appreciated some detailed explanation. There are certain arrangements and items for worship described in vs 2–5a but the author says, 'we cannot discuss these things in detail now' (v 5). This is because the major teaching significance of the tabernacle arrangements, and especially those about entering the 'Most

Holy Place' (v 8), is purely negative. Only the high priest could enter the Most Holy Place and then only once a year on the Day of Atonement and with the need to atone for his and the people's sins. From this the writer draws the lesson that while the first tabernacle still stood, the way to draw near to God was not yet disclosed (v 8).

The sanctuary where Christ entered to present his offering is 'heaven itself' (9:24), which is described as, 'the greater and more perfect tabernacle that is not man-made, that is to say, not a part of this creation' (9:11). That the writers of elaborate books on the typology of the tabernacle are not entirely barking up the wrong tree is shown in the fact that the Levitical priests 'serve at a sanctuary that is a copy and shadow of what is in heaven. That is why Moses was warned when he was about to build the tabernacle: "See to it that you make everything according to the pattern shown you on the mountain"' (8:5). In some shadowy way the spiritual realities of access to God in heaven are pictured for us in the old covenant tabernacle and temple. However the lessons we must learn about the tabernacle are that, 'the way into the Most Holy Place had not yet been disclosed' (9:8) and, 'the gifts and sacrifices being offered were not able to clear the conscience of the worshipper' (9:9).

The accomplishment of Christ's sacrifice

GOD'S PLAN AND CHRIST'S DEATH

Before we look at what is achieved by Christ's offering in any detail, it is important to remember that the offering takes place as a result of God's gracious and loving plan. This is clear in such basic gospel texts as John 3:16 and is also the perspective of the writer to the Hebrews. An often-made objection to evangelical presentations of the gospel is that the impression given is of a compassionate Saviour winning blessings through his death from a reluctant Father. That we are not to think like this is clear from one verse alone in Hebrews, 'so that by the grace of God he might taste death for everyone' (2:9). John Calvin writes, 'there is added that this is done by the grace of God, because the ground of our redemption is that immense love of God towards us by which it happened that he did not spare his own son.'[3] Again in 10:7, Christ coming into the world says (quoting

Psalm 40:8), 'I have come to do your will, O God.' It is 'by that will, we have been made holy through the sacrifice of the body of Jesus Christ once for all' (10:10). It is only within the context of the grace and plan of God that we can rightly consider the death of Christ.

Looking through what is written about Christ's sacrifice in the passage from 9:11–10:18 there are three major deficiencies of the old covenant sacrifices that are remedied and made up for by Christ's sacrifice. The old covenant sacrifices cannot cleanse the conscience of guilt but Christ's sacrifice can. The old covenant sacrifices had therefore to be repeated year in and year out but Christ's offering is once for all. Until the sins committed under the old covenant were paid for, that covenant had to remain in force but Christ's sacrifice deals with all sin; past, present and future.

THE PROBLEM OF THE CONSCIENCE

He did not enter by means of the blood of goats and calves; but he entered the Most Holy Place once for all by his own blood, having obtained eternal redemption. The blood of goats and bulls and the ashes of a heifer sprinkled on those who are ceremonially unclean sanctify them so that they are outwardly clean. How much more, then, will the blood of Christ, who through the eternal Spirit offered himself unblemished to God, cleanse our consciences from acts that lead to death, so that we may serve the living God! (Hebrews 9:12–14)

[1]The law is only a shadow of the good things that are coming—not the realities themselves. For this reason it can never, by the same sacrifices repeated endlessly year after year, make perfect those who draw near to worship. [2]If it could, would they not have stopped being offered? For the worshippers would have been cleansed once for all, and would no longer have felt guilty for their sins. [3]But those sacrifices are an annual reminder of sins, [4]because it is impossible for the blood of bulls and goats to take away sins. [5]Therefore, when Christ came into the world, he said:

'Sacrifice and offering you did not desire,
but a body you prepared for me;
[6]with burnt offerings and sin offerings you were not pleased.
[7]Then I said, 'Here I am—it is written about me in the scroll—
I have come to do your will, O God.'

[8]First he said, 'Sacrifices and offerings, burnt offerings and sin offerings you did not desire, nor were you pleased with them' (although the law required them to be made). [9]Then he said, 'Here I am, I have come to do your will.' He sets aside the first to establish the second. [10]And by that will, we have been made holy through the sacrifice of the body of Jesus Christ once for all (Hebrews 10:1–10).

The writer is completely attuned to the realities of the old covenant sacrifices. What they could do is offer a cleansing which satisfied the need to provide ritual cleaning so that people could take part in the worship of the tabernacle or temple (9:13). What they could not do is to cleanse the conscience for 'it is impossible for the blood of bulls and goats to take away sins' (10:4). In fact the writer says that if the old covenant sacrifices could 'make perfect those who draw near to worship' (10:1) by producing a situation where 'the worshippers would have been cleansed once for all, and would no longer have felt guilty for their sins' (10:2) then they 'would … have stopped being offered.' (10:2) Their continued existence simply provides an eloquent testimony that they cannot finally deal with sin or conscience (10:3). Their cessation will demonstrate that an effective sacrifice has been found. Therefore the validity of the Old Testament sacrifices ceased with Christ's death. However it is also a noteworthy fact of history that within a lifetime (AD 70) the sacrifices were actually brought to an end by the destruction of the temple.

Thinking about his own sin and then considering the sacrifices being offered left the reflective old covenant worshipper unsatisfied by the provision being made. How could the worshipper see the death of an animal and feel it fully dealt with his guilt? Though it is an unpleasant thought, how would you feel if a family pet were sacrificed for your sins? I think how I would feel if either our pet greyhound Willow, or Miss Whiskas the cat we used to own, were to be a sacrificial victim for my sins. One lesson I would be very conscious of is a sense of the cost of sin and the loss involved in sacrifice. However I would also be quite clear that the death could not realistically cover my guilt in any way.

Christ's sacrifice of course is capable of fully and appropriately atoning for sin and hence can provide cleansing for the conscience. In 9:13–14 the writer reasons from the known, the acknowledged effectiveness of the old covenant sacrifices, to the truths about Christ's sacrifice that the Hebrew Christians have to be established in. He uses the same sort of, 'how much more' argument that Jesus used in talking to his disciples about worrying about clothes.4 In this case the appeal is to the fact that under the old covenant the sacrifices of the day of atonement5 (v 13), 'the blood of bulls and goats' and the purifying water6 made with 'the ashes of a heifer' were effective in providing a ritual and ceremonial cleanliness that enabled participation in old covenant worship.

In contrast, Christ's 'blood' (v 14), by which we mean his sacrificial death, is superior in two ways. Firstly by its own nature, because he, 'through the eternal Spirit offered himself'—it is a freely, intelligently and willingly given sacrifice. In addition he 'offered himself unblemished,' which means not physical perfection, as with the sacrifices mentioned in v 13, but moral purity and acceptability to God; the God, who does not look at the outward appearance, but at the heart (1 Samuel 16:7). Secondly it is superior in its effects because, instead of outward cleansing, which gave ceremonial cleanness, it was able to, 'cleanse our consciences from acts that lead to [literally 'of'] death so that we may serve the living God.' The conscience, our ability to think back on our own actions and see them as right or wrong, is set free because an adequate sacrifice is now available. The result is that in every aspect of our lives (see Romans 12:1) we may now offer religious service, that is spiritual worship, to God. Isaac Watts wrote:

Not all the blood of beasts,
On Jewish altars slain,
Could give the guilty conscience peace,
Or wash away the stain.

This states the problem. Charles Wesley gives the solution when he wrote:

Jesus, my great High Priest,
Offered his blood and died;
My guilty conscience seeks
No sacrifice beside;7

In 10:5–10 the writer develops the point of the superiority of Christ's offering. The writer quotes Psalm 40:6–8 to indicate that the animal sacrifices, though required by the law (v 8), were replaced by Christ's offering of himself. His obedience in life and to a once for all sacrificial death replaces the old covenant sacrifices and secures a status as (v 10), 'holy' for God's people. Under the old covenant sacrifice without obedience was anathema to God. The Lord says (Hosea 6:6), 'I desire mercy [a broad term that denotes the whole life of obedient response to God's covenantal grace] not [rather than] sacrifice.' In the new covenant the willing and obedient sacrifice of Christ does away with all other sacrifices.

It is important that we relate the sacrificial death of Jesus to the exercise of his Priesthood. For, not only is his sacrifice seen to be an act of worship but also it is the highest act of worship. JH Thornwell writes:

He was a priest in his death, a priest in his resurrection, a priest in his ascension. He worshipped God in laying his life upon the altar, he worshipped him in taking it again, and it was an act of worship by which he entered with his blood into the very presence of the Highest to intercede for the saints.[8]

Writing of the cross in particular he writes:

Every groan and pang, every exclamation of agony, amazement and horror, was a homage to God which, in itself considered, the Priest felt it glorious to render. ... In this aspect the satisfaction of Jesus is not merely the ground on which others are at liberty to approach and adore the Divine perfections; it is itself a prayer uttered by the lips of one whose deeds were words—a hymn of praise chanted by him whose songs were the inspiration of holiness and truth.[9]

The need for a once for all sacrifice

The writer to the Hebrews has already made the point that if a sacrifice could offer once for all cleansing and a clean conscience then sacrifices would cease. This is in fact the case for 'he has appeared once for all at the end of the ages to do away with sin by the sacrifice of himself' (9:26). Jesus' continuing work is intercession, not sacrifice. The next epoch in his high priestly ministry will be to emerge from the true tabernacle to 'bring salvation to those who are waiting for him' (9:28) .

This picture is drawn from the Day of Atonement when the emergence of the high priest from the inner sanctuary showed everyone that the sacrifice had been accepted. The Hebrew Christians had experienced it, and we can imagine the tension and then the relief as the high priest reappeared with sin dealt with for another year! Although the acceptance of Christ's sacrifice is shown by the resurrection, the final and glorious confirmation will be his second coming. Until then we live by faith but then we will see the sacrifice's acceptance and efficacy confirmed. FF Bruce writes:

This presentation of the return of Christ in terms of the high priest's emergence from the sanctuary was in Frances Ridley Havergal's mind when she wrote:

> Coming! In the opening east
> Herald brightness slowly swells;
> Coming! O my glorious Priest,
> Hear we not thy golden bells?[10]

Of course the important question is whether we will be among those found waiting in eager anticipation when Jesus does return? This of course focuses the pastoral concern of the writer to the Hebrews that they should continue faithful and not fall away.

Day after day every priest stands and performs his religious duties; again and again he offers the same sacrifices, which can never take away sins. But when this priest had offered for all time one sacrifice for sins, he sat down at the right hand of God. Since that time he waits for his enemies to be made his footstool, because by one sacrifice he has made perfect for ever those who are being made holy (Hebrews 10:11–14).

These verses summarise the teaching on Christ's sacrifice by contrasting between the Old Covenant priests and their sacrifices and Christ and his sacrifice. We can best see this by putting the two priesthoods and sacrifices in different columns.

The Aaronic priests and sacrifices	Christ and his sacrifice
'Day after day … again and again he offers the same sacrifices'	'offered for all time one sacrifice for sins'
'stands and performs his religious duties'	'sat down at the right hand of God. Since that time he waits for his enemies to be made his footstool'
'sacrifices which can never take away sins'	'by one sacrifice he has made perfect for ever those who are being made holy.'

It is of the greatest importance to the writer that the current ministry of intercession carried out by Jesus is enabled by his completed sacrificial work.

Christ's death brings in the new covenant

[15]For this reason Christ is the mediator of a new covenant, that those who are called may receive the promised eternal inheritance—now that he has died as a ransom to set them free from the sins committed under the first covenant. [16]In the case of a will, it is necessary to prove the death of the one who made it, [17]because a will is in force only when somebody has died; it never takes effect while the one who made it is living. [18]This is why even the first covenant was not put into effect without blood. [19]When Moses had proclaimed every commandment of the law to all the people, he took the blood of calves, together with water, scarlet wool and branches of hyssop, and sprinkled the scroll and all the people. [20]He said, 'This is the blood of the covenant, which God has commanded you to keep.' [21]In the same way, he sprinkled with the blood both the tabernacle and everything used in its ceremonies. [22]In fact, the law requires that nearly everything be cleansed with blood, and without the shedding of blood there is no forgiveness. [23]It was necessary, then, for the copies of the heavenly things to be purified with these sacrifices, but the heavenly things themselves with better sacrifices than these. [24]For Christ did not enter a man-made sanctuary that was only a copy of the true one; he entered heaven itself, now to appear for us in God's presence. [25]Nor did he enter heaven to offer himself again and again, the way the high priest enters the Most Holy Place every year with blood that is not his own. [26]Then Christ would have had to suffer many times since the creation of the world. But now he

has appeared once for all at the end of the ages to do away with sin by the sacrifice of himself. [27]Just as man is destined to die once, and after that to face judgment, [28]so Christ was sacrificed once to take away the sins of many people; and he will appear a second time, not to bear sin, but to bring salvation to those who are waiting for him (Hebrews 9:15–28).

The problem in bringing in the new covenant is that the sins dealt with by the animal sacrifices of the old covenant had never been fully paid for. So, like an undischarged bankrupt who cannot start a new business until his old debts are honoured, God's people were left under the old covenant arrangements until the sacrifice of Christ. Only with the provision of a sufficient and final sacrifice for sins can the new covenant be inaugurated.

Jesus is now the mediator of the new covenant and guarantees the eternal inheritance to the called (v 15a). This can be so because his death is 'a ransom to set them free from the sins committed under the first covenant' (v 15b). Clearly his sacrifice works backwards in time as well as forwards (see Romans 3:25). DA Hagner writes: 'forgiveness experienced during the OT period depended finally—although this was hardly understood at the time—upon an event that was to take place in the future. The sacrifice of Christ is the answer to sin in every era, past and present, since it alone is the means of forgiveness.'[11]

9:16–22 is a notoriously difficult passage to interpret. The area of debate is over whether 'diatheke', the Greek word translated 'covenant' elsewhere in Hebrews, should be translated as 'will' in vs 16, 17. I take the view that the topic of vs 15–17 is covenant making and confirmation, not the making and executing of a will. It seems very unlikely that the meaning of a crucial term would be changed halfway through a section of careful argument and reasoning and a perfectly good and clear explanation of the passage, in terms of covenant making and confirmation rather than the making of a will, has been put forward.[12] We are to understand that covenant making involves invoking covenant curses on disobedience. The occasion on which this is most graphically symbolised in Scripture is in Genesis 15:9–21 where the covenant making ceremony involved passing between the dismembered animals. Symbolically the covenant makers are saying, 'Let the same thing happen to me if I do not keep the covenant conditions!' It is very significant, as regards who will bear the covenant curses, that in Genesis 15 only the LORD (in visionary form) passed between the pieces.

What the writer is clearly teaching is that Christ's death involved taking upon himself the covenant curses and penalties. These are elaborated at great length in Deuteronomy 28:16–28. Christ has received the covenant penalty of death, which was symbolised in the covenant making ceremony described in vs 18–22. The same idea is developed in Galatians 3:13 where we read, 'Christ redeemed us from the curse of the law by becoming a curse for us, for it is written: "Cursed is everyone who is hung on a tree."' Having satisfied all the outstanding claims of the old covenant, Jesus is in a position to bring in the new covenant.

9:23–28 move on from the old covenant ratification ceremony to new covenant ratification. We move from (v 23), 'copies of the heavenly things' to 'the heavenly things themselves': from (v 24), 'a man-made sanctuary' to 'heaven itself' and 'God's presence': from (vs 25–26) repeated sacrifices of animals to an appearance 'once for all at the end of the ages to do away with sin by the sacrifice of himself.' In vs 27–28 the writer moves from the ceremonies of the old covenant to a general truth about humanity, that we die once and then experience judgement. Christ therefore could only die once to deal with the 'sins of many people' and he has received a positive judgement when his sacrifice was accepted. Therefore his second appearance and coming will be 'not to bear sin, but to bring salvation to those who are waiting for him.'

Moving to the heart of the matter

Like the reality of Christ's humanity, the significance and finality of the sacrifice of Christ is of great importance to the writer to the Hebrews. It is not however the centre of his message. Like everything else it is explained to serve his central theme, which is Christ's current intercession and therefore ability to send help in time of need. It is to this subject we now turn in the next three chapters.

Notes

1 **Isaac Watts,** *Join all the glorious names.*

2 **H Seeseman,** *Theological Dictionary of the New Testament,* ed. G. Kittel and G. Friedrich, Eerdmans, 1985.

3 **John Calvin,** *Commentary on the Epistle of Paul to the Hebrews,* St Andrews Press, 1963, p. 24.

4 Matthew 6:25–27.

5 See Leviticus 16.

6 See Numbers 19.

7 **Charles Wesley,** *Join all the glorious names.*

8 **JH Thornwell,** *Collected Writings,* volume 2, original publication 1875, Banner of Truth, 1974, pp. 280–281.

9 **JH Thornwell,** *op. cit.,* p. 280.

10 **FF Bruce,** *New International Commentary on Hebrews,* Eerdmans. 1962, p. 224. Quoting the hymn: *Thou art coming, O my Saviour.*

11 **Donald A Hagner,** *New International Bible Commentary on Hebrews,* Hendrickson, 1983, p. 141.

12 This view is reflected in the *New American Standard Bible* and defended in **William Lane,** *Word Bible Commentary on Hebrews,* 1991, note p on p. 231. **O Palmer Robertson,** *The Christ of the Covenants,* Presbyterian & Reformed, 1980, develops this understanding in detail on pp. 138–144. Lane translates vs 15–17: 'And for this reason he is the mediator of a new covenant, in order that, a death having occurred for redemption from transgressions committed on the basis of the former covenant, those who are called might receive the promised eternal inheritance. (For where there is a covenant, it is necessary for the death of the one who ratifies it to be brought forward, for a covenant is made legally secure on the basis of the sacrificial victims, since it is never valid while the ratifier lives.)'.

Christ's intercession (1)

Before the throne of God above
I have a strong, a perfect plea,
A great High Priest, whose name is Love,
Who ever lives and pleads for me.[1]

The importance of knowing about Christ's intercession

We all know that it should never be so but sometimes, when we are feeling down and overwhelmed by pressures and difficulties, the gospel and Christ's sacrificial death for us seem very remote from us. We would love to know what it is that Jesus is doing now to help us in our time of need and to sustain us in our Christian faith. The Hebrew Christians could identify with us in this because they feel alone, unloved and orphaned. They feel as though God does not care and cannot or will not intervene in their situation. It is precisely to this feeling and this spiritual need that the writer to the Hebrews wants to respond.

In the previous chapters we have looked at the way in which Jesus fulfils the position of High Priest for his people. He is properly appointed by God to a superior order of priesthood, that of Melchizedek. He is able to sympathise in the experience of temptation as well as the experience of suffering. He has offered a once-for-all sacrifice that deals completely with his people's sins. What then remains for Jesus to do? The remaining task is spoken of in Hebrews 7:25, 'he is able to save completely [and for ever] those who come to God through him, because he always lives to intercede for them.' This ability to bring help into his readers' situation is the centre of the concern of the writer to the Hebrews. Having established the truths that we looked at in chapters three to seven, the writer is in a position not only to say that Jesus cares but that he intervenes by interceding and sending help. The result sought is that we will now believe that we can turn confidently to him in prayer expecting he will supply mercy and grace for our time of need. JC Ryle writes: 'If we are true Christians we shall find it essential to our comfort in religion to have clear views of Christ's priestly office and intercession. Christ lives, and therefore our faith shall not fail.'[2]

In this chapter, we will look firstly at the picture of the intercession of Christ as we find it in the work of the high priest under the Old Covenant. Secondly we will look at the New Testament picture of Christ's work in intercession as we find it outside the book of Hebrews. Thirdly we will begin to look at the distinctive contribution that the book of Hebrews makes to our understanding of Christ's intercession.

The high priestly work of intercession in the Old Testament

It is important to remember that the writer is able to assume a background of knowledge when he speaks about Jesus interceding for us as our great high priest. This is because the high priest in the Old Testament was seen as having a ministry of intercession and many of his readers will have attended the great religious festivals in Jerusalem. The task the High Priest had was 'to represent them [the people] in matters related to God' (Hebrews 5:1). This did not only consist of the fact that he was the one to 'offer gifts and sacrifices for sins' but included a work of intercession. This stemmed from the access to the most holy place gained through sacrifice. While Jesus' intercession in God's presence is based on greater and more effective sacrifices, and on his own immortality, there is still a link between the two priesthoods—that of Jesus and that of Aaron. Jesus' work is seen as casting its shadow back into the Old Testament period in that the Old Testament practices were designed to point to his coming and his accomplishments for his people.

THE DAY OF ATONEMENT

The passage where the high priest's work of intercession is most clearly set before us is in Leviticus 16 where the regulations for the Day of Atonement are set out. The significance of the details of the ritual are symbolic, as fits in with the Old Covenant period, rather than set out explicitly. Interestingly in Hebrews 9:3 and 4 we read, 'Behind the second curtain was a room called the Most Holy Place, which had the golden altar of incense and the gold-covered ark of the covenant.' Strangely the altar of incense is outside the second curtain in the Holy Place and not inside the Most Holy Place. The writer is not making a mistake in details but making the point that the altar of incense is immediately outside the Most Holy Place and it is used as the high priest enters 'behind the curtain' (Leviticus 16:12). So the altar of incense is so intimately linked with the Most Holy Place as to be regarded as part of it. It is also closely linked with the daily ministry of the high priest who burns incense morning and evening before the LORD (Exodus 30:7). The incense, whose smoke ascending skywards represents intercessory prayer according to New Testament understanding (Luke 1:10 and Revelation 8:3–4), accompanies the offer of a bull as a sin offering for Aaron's family (Leviticus 16:11). The same pattern appears to apply to the sin offering for the people in Leviticus 16:15–16. It is the sacrifice and intercession combined that succeed in applying forgiveness of sins to God's people. Patrick Fairbairn writes: 'the high priest, the head and representative of a sin-stricken community, going under the felt load of innumerable transgressions into the earthly presence-chamber of Jehovah; [is] permitted to stand there in peace and safety, because entering with the incense of devout supplication and the blood of an acceptable sacrifice.'3

THE HIGH PRIEST AS HIS PEOPLE'S REPRESENTATIVE

The work of the high priest is performed as a representative of the people of God. This is made very plain in the obvious symbolism of the high priestly clothes made for him. The ephod has two onyx stones mounted on its shoulder pieces and on them are engraved the names of the twelve tribes of Israel in order of their birth (see Exodus 28:6–14). The breast-piece (Exodus 28:15–30) has on it twelve precious stones, each in gold filigree settings and with the name of one of the tribes of Israel on it. The reason for this is quite explicit, 'Whenever Aaron enters the Holy Place, he will bear the names of the sons of Israel over his heart on the breast-piece of decision as a continuing memorial before the LORD' (v 29). So in all his high priestly ministrations the idea of the high priest representing the people before the Lord and reminding him of their needs is prominent.

On the Day of Atonement the high priest, rather than wearing his glorious and kingly clothing, appears in simple white linen (Leviticus 16:3–4). He enters God's presence and must do so as servant rather than king. It is a reminder that there he represents his brothers as one of them.

The details of the Day of Atonement are not easy to grasp but it seems that the high priest leaves the people as king and becomes servant, through changing his clothing, as he passes through the Holy Place on to his way into the presence of God, then again changes back in the Holy Place to his glorious priestly robes before he again comes before the people.

Christ's present work of intercession as seen in the New Testament

IN THE NEW TESTAMENT OTHER THAN IN THE BOOK OF HEBREWS

We are going to look at the passages that indicate the Lord Jesus has an ongoing work of intercession for us in glory rather than those that refer to his life of prayer on earth. The reasons for this are firstly because no one disputes that Jesus habitually prayed on earth 'Jesus often withdrew to lonely places and prayed' (Luke 5:16). However the question of the active nature of his intercession in glory is disputed. Secondly we are reserving until chapter 10 an examination of the records of Jesus' earthly intercessions as giving us indications as to the pattern of his heavenly intercession. There are two New Testament references to his work of interceding for us—Romans 8:34 and 1 John 2:2.

In the passage where we find our first reference, Paul is dealing with the problem of Christians suffering and feeling they could be cut off from God's love in Christ:

31What, then, shall we say in response to this? If God is for us, who can be against us? 32He who did not spare his own Son, but gave him up for us all—how will he not also, along with him, graciously give us all things? 33Who will bring any charge against those whom God has chosen? It is God who justifies. 34Who is he that condemns? Christ Jesus, who died—more than that, who was raised to life—is at the right hand of God and is also interceding for us. 35Who shall separate us from the love of Christ? (Romans 8:31–35)

The passage then moves on to its triumphant conclusion that nothing in all creation 'will be able to separate us from the love of God which is in Christ Jesus our Lord' (8:39).

The problem the Roman Christians are facing in this passage appears to be the fear that suffering indicates God's displeasure. Therefore suffering would mean we are in danger of experiencing condemnation and hence separation from God's love. The answer is firstly that, 'the Spirit helps us in our weakness … because the Spirit intercedes for the saints in accordance with God's will' (8:26–27). This refers to the fact that the Spirit aids our own prayer even when that prayer is reduced to inarticulate groans to God. This establishes the subjective fact that even when we feel at our lowest, God does not abandon us.

Verses 28ff. take up the more objective question: not how will we cope in our circumstances but what is God actually doing in our circumstances? Verses 28–30 explain the glorious purposes God is working out for his people. If we are, 'called according to his purpose' then the whole process of foreknowledge to being 'glorified' will be fulfilled in our experience. Verses 31 and 34 deal with the conclusions we draw from this—that, 'God is for us' then we know that he will provide all we need to bring us through to glorification. Verses 33–34 deal with the fact that we cannot fall back into condemnation and therefore become separated from God's love. There can be no charge against us or condemnation for us with God as the one, 'who justifies' and Jesus 'who died … who was raised to life' and who is now 'at the right hand of God and is also interceding for us.' In this context of accusation and condemnation it would appear that the intercession means that 'he continues to secure for his people the benefit of his death.'[4]

Our second reference shows the apostle John dealing with Christ's present intercession for his people: 'My dear children, I write this to you so that you will not sin. But if anyone does sin we have one who speaks to the Father in our defence—Jesus Christ the Righteous One' (1 John 2:1). It should be pointed out here that the word paraphrased in the NIV as 'one who speaks to the Father in our defence' is not the word translated as 'intercede' in Romans and Hebrews. It is the word 'paraclete' which literally means, 'one called alongside in order to help' and in the context in 1 John, 'undoubtedly signifies an "advocate" or "counsel for the defence" in a legal context.'[5] The idea is that, though we have nothing to plead with God that could excuse or cover our sins, Jesus is able to plead his own righteousness and his atoning death for our sins on our behalf. This would fit with the position explained by Charles Hodge that, 'he continues to secure for his people the benefit of his death'[4] in the sense that he continues to secure our justification and our right standing before God.

CHRIST'S INTERCESSION IN THE BOOK OF HEBREWS

In 1 John the meaning of Christ's intercession appears to be completely thought of in forensic terms. In other words we are concerned entirely with the matter of right standing with God. In Romans as well, this appears to be the predominant thought though there does appear to be a subsidiary thought in the surrounding context that this then secures the 'all things' (Romans 8:32) that are necessary to enable our continuance in the Christian life despite suffering. In the book of Hebrews the focus seems to change somewhat. The concern is less with justification than with being able to 'draw near to God' (7:19). However, even accepting that the legal idea of justification is not totally out of the picture, either in Hebrews 7:25 or in Hebrews 4:14–16, the focus is mainly on the high priestly work of intercession securing the 'grace to help us in our time of need' and providing what is needed for our complete and eternal salvation. In other words we are looking at something which is more to do with life than with the law court. Hebrews is building on the teaching of the rest of the New Testament and is encouraging us to see that not only our right standing with God but also the grace provided to ensure our continuing in faith, rest on Christ's intercession for us.

What does it mean to say that Christ intercedes for us?

Before we move on to consider in more detail what is won for us through Christ's work of intercession, and what that continuing work of intercession on our behalf means for us, we need to consider an important question. The question we need to address is: what is the nature of Christ's intercession? This is a much debated point theologically and the question is, 'How is this [intercession] to be construed? Is it secured merely by his presence there as a man, or is he actually praying to the Father for his people?'[6] As a matter of convenience we can refer to these positions as presence-intercession and petition-intercession.

PRESENCE INTERCESSION

It has to be said that many eminent Christian leaders and teachers hold the understanding that the intercession consists of Christ's presence in heaven. In the last century Charles Hodge, representing the Princeton School of Theology, and the great Biblical commentator BF Westcott both held to it. Additionally the two leading evangelical ministers in England during the second half of the 20th Century, John Stott and Dr Martyn Lloyd-Jones, take this view.

Dr Lloyd-Jones, in his discussion of this issue, emphasises the way in which some of the Puritans and their followers over-dramatised the concept of intercession in their preaching:

God the judge was sitting on the bench, and there was counsel for the prosecution, the devil, and defending counsel, our advocate the Lord Jesus Christ. The court was in session and our adversary the Devil and accuser was bringing his charge and trying to prove it. But the Lord Jesus Christ got up and answered the charge; and God, having heard the defence, pronounced his verdict.7

Dr Lloyd-Jones then goes on to quote Charles Hodge with great approval: 'Of course this language is figurative; the meaning is, that Christ continues since His resurrection and exaltation to secure for his people the benefits of his death. Everything comes from God through him and for his sake.'7 The comment is added: 'That is precisely what it means. It cannot carry the other meaning.'

CRITIQUE OF PRESENCE INTERCESSION

I think the arguments for this position are far from compelling. Firstly those who advocate this sometimes appear to be reacting to an alternative view, which is quite extreme, and is actually a straw man, which no one would defend exegetically. That is certainly the case with Dr Lloyd-Jones and it would be more convincing if a more guarded and carefully nuanced view of intercession was put up as the alternative view. Secondly, while presence intercession might be a perfectly reasonable, and possibly adequate, explanation for 1 John 2:1–2, and even possibly for Romans 8:34, this explanation does not cover the rather wider concept of intercession contained in the book of Hebrews. Thirdly, to say that the language is figurative is misleading because this view empties the concept of intercession of any real meaning. According to this understanding there is *no activity actually taking place which is involved in the intercession* and Christ's presence constitutes all that can be put under the heading of intercession.

When we are dealing with such concepts as intercession, biblical language is to be regarded as analogous rather than figurative. By this we mean that the terminology properly understood points to the fact that there is an activity going on which closely resembles, and can be described as intercession, though it is not entirely identical to our own activity of intercession. HH Meeter, in his thorough study of Christ's Priesthood, writes: 'We cannot ... say with Westcott that Christ intercedes by his mere presence on the Father's throne. There is a specific activity relating to the *entygchanein* (intercession).'[8]

Cautions concerning petition intercession

We have to accept that Christ's intercession is analogous but not identical to ours and there are a number of reasons for this. Even on earth the Saviour's activity in prayer was not identical to our own—for example at Lazarus' tomb he says 'Father, I thank you that you have heard me. I knew that you always hear me' (John 11:41). DA Carson comments: 'the prayer assumes that Jesus has already asked the Father for Lazarus' life, and that all he must do is to thank his Father for the answer.'[9] Additionally great emphasis is put on the finished nature of Christ's work in the book of Hebrews. This starts as early as Hebrews 1:3, 'After he had provided purification for sins, he sat down at the right hand of the Majesty in heaven.' This is put in contrast to other priests who continue to serve day after day offering the same sacrifices. 'But when this priest had offered for all time one sacrifice for sins, he sat down at the right hand of God.' (10:12) With this emphasis so strong it is understandable that Protestant writers have felt that an emphasis on the idea of Christ praying for his people in heaven would be misleading, particularly if this activity of ongoing prayer and intercession is linked to the thought of his sacrifice being continually re-presented to his Father.

THE CASE FOR PETITION INTERCESSION

In reply to the case for presence intercession it has to be said that this approach actually robs the reader of the book of Hebrews of some of the most substantial encouragement on offer. The concept of Jesus as a sympathetic High Priest actually and actively interceding for his people, which we take to include praying for them, is central to the purpose of the writer. Our task, whilst taking on board the genuine difficulties, is to understand what the writer to the Hebrews intended his readers to believe.

In seeking an accurate understanding of the idea of intercession we will find that, far from uniformly adopting the position of BF Westcott, Charles Hodge, DM Lloyd-Jones and JRW Stott, the evangelical world has had many respected teachers who have maintained that Christ's intercession does actually involve him praying. This does not mean that intercession only involves praying, the term used is rather wider in its meaning, but that prayer is rightly regarded as being included in the intercession. Those supporting this understanding include John Calvin from the 16th Century, John Owen from the 17th Century, RL Dabney and JH Thornwell from the 19th Century and Louis Berkhof and Wayne Grudem in the 20th Century. Wayne Grudem writes:

This view [intercession by virtue of his presence in heaven] does not fit the actual language used in Romans 8:34 and Hebrews 7:25. In both cases the word 'intercede' translates the Greek term *entygchano*. This word does not mean merely 'to stand as someone's representative before another person,' but clearly has the sense of making specific requests or petitions before someone.[10]

The two major writers on this subject, William Milligan and HH Meeter, interpret the term as meaning: 'to transact with one person with reference to another'[11] and Milligan adds: 'either by making a statement concerning him upon which certain proceedings ought to follow, or asking something "for" him or "against" him.' We are to be very cautious in going beyond this but clearly simple presence does not correspond to what is meant by intercession. HH Meeter again expresses this carefully: 'All that we can say is that [the intercession] is an uninterrupted activity of the enthroned High Priest at the right hand of God as high priestly mediator for his covenant people, through which he invokes for them from God the Father the blessings of salvation.'[12] Milligan warns against a narrowing of the idea to prayer alone and also links Christ's intercession to his appearance as High Priest in Revelation 1 where: 'he "knows" them [the churches] in order that he may furnish them with supplies of strength and guidance which their ever-varying circumstances require. He that walks in the midst of the seven golden candlesticks keeps them, and trims them, and pours fresh oil into them, that they may shine with undimmed brightness in the sanctuary.'13 This broadening of the concept means that all Christ's activity in regard to his people as obtaining for them the Father's blessing is seen as coming under this head. The reservation that I have about this broadening of the concept is that the idea of intercession in Hebrews is quite explicitly linked to Christ's office and activity as High Priest. In Revelation 1 the figure who is described as 'dressed in a robe reaching down to his feet and with a golden sash round his chest' (v 13) is pictured as explicitly priestly. However unless an activity of Christ is shown to be explicitly priestly I question whether it can rightly be put under the head of intercession. So we should consider the main focus of our understanding of Jesus' intercession to be a ministry of prayer. To deny this seems to fly in the face of the obvious meaning of Scripture.

OBJECTIONS TO PETITION INTERCESSION ANSWERED

The main difficulties relate to the finished nature of Christ's work, to the idea that it would be dishonouring to the Father to suppose he needs persuasion to be gracious, and to the interpretation of John 16:26–27. As regards the finished nature of Christ's work we have to accept the paradox the metaphorical and analogical language of Scripture brings. A recent article sums up the paradoxes involved very succinctly: 'Though ceaselessly active in heaven as our Prophet, Priest and King, he is at the same time resting from his sacrificial work on earth.'14

John Murray deals with the objections to teaching Christ's continued activity of prayer. Particularly the objections based on the idea that it is 'a reflection on the knowledge, love and beneficence of the Father to suppose that solicitation on the part of Christ is necessary to the bestowments of grace of which the Father is the agent.' He points out that we must take 'all the data of revelation into account when we think of Jesus' heavenly ministry.'15 His conclusion is:

There is an indestructible relationship between the economical arrangement whereby Jesus intercedes with the Father in heaven and the concrete facts of Jesus' humiliation as the servant of the Father. If it were not dishonouring to the Father to send his own Son into this world, it is not dishonouring for the Father to act now in the progressive realisation of his saving counsel through a mediation which the Son exercises through the mode of intercession.[16]

This means that biblically we are right to insist that God's love for us is expressed to us, not won for us, by Christ's death on the cross (John 3:16). The same logic then applies to God's provision of an interceding high priest—this provision expresses the Father's love to us and provides the means by which he will pour his blessings into our lives. Jesus' presence and intercession is certainly not needed to persuade the Father to love us but becomes the expression and channel of the Father's love. DA Carson writes:

Even if our great high priest intercedes for us and pleads his own blood on our behalf, we must never think of this as an independent action that the Father did not know about or reluctantly approved, eventually won over by the independently originating sacrifice of his Son. Rather, Father and Son are one in this project of redemption. The Son himself comes into the world by the express command of the Father.[17]

A final objection to the view that Jesus is actively praying for us in heaven is found in the words of John 16:26–27, 'In that day you will ask in my name. I am not saying that I will ask the Father on your behalf. No, the Father himself loves you because you have loved me and have believed that I came from God.' Properly understood, Jesus is assuring his disciples that, 'the Father himself loves you' and that he, Jesus, will not function as a sort of go-between to whom they must go in order to pray. To pray in Jesus' name means that they have access freely into God's presence. This of course is the teaching of Hebrews 4:16 where believers are invited to, 'approach the throne of grace with confidence'. DA Carson writes concerning John 16:26–27:

Nor is this truth in conflict with New Testament passages that emphasise the intercessory work of the exalted Christ … Rightly understood, such passages focus on the mediatorial role of the Son in the plan of redemption, and therefore on the basis of the Christian's acceptance by God; they do not stipulate a mechanical conveyancing of the Christian's prayers, as if Jesus' purpose was to restrict the believer's access to the Father.[18]

Moving on

We have now established what is meant by Christ's intercession. This means we can now go on in our next chapter to examine what he intercedes for and the encouragement we are now to draw from his intercession.

Notes

1 **Charities Lees De Chenez,** *Before the throne of God above.*

2 **JC Ryle,** *Expository Thoughts on the Gospels-Luke,* volume 2, William Hunt and Co., 1874, p. 412.

3 **Patrick Fairbairn,** *The Typology of Scripture,* Guardian Press, 1975, Vol. 2 (2 vols. in one), p. 343.

4 **John Stott,** *The Message of Romans,* IVP, 1994, p. 290.

5 **I Howard Marshall,** *New International Commentary on the Epistles of John,* Eerdmans, 1978, p. 116.

6 **JP Baker,** *New Dictionary of Theology,* IVP, 1988, p. 477.

7 **D Martyn Lloyd-Jones,** *Exposition of Romans 8:17–39—The Final Perseverance of the Saints,* Banner of Truth, 1975, p. 435.

8 **HH Meeter,** *The Heavenly High Priesthood of Christ,* Eerdmans, p. 183.

9 **D A Carson,** *The Gospel according to John,* IVP, 1991, p. 418.

10 **Wayne Grudem,** *Systematic Theology,* IVP, 1994, p. 627.

11 **HH Meeter,** *op. cit.,* and **William Milligan,** *The Ascension and Heavenly Priesthood of Our Lord,* MacMillan, 1908, p. 151.

12 **HH Meeter,** *op. cit.,* p. 184.

13 **William Milligan,** *op. cit.,* p. 157.

14 **David Campbell,** *The Cross—its perfect triumph,* Evangelical Times, June 2000, p. 14.

15 **John Murray,** *Collected Writings—Volume 1,* Banner of Truth, 1976, p. 52.

16 **John Murray,** *op. cit.,* p. 53.

17 **DA Carson,** *The Difficult Doctrine of the Love of God,* IVP, 2000, pp. 82–83.

18 **DA Carson,** *op. cit.,* p. 547.

Christ's intercession (2)

We have a hope
which is steadfast and certain,
gone through the curtain
and touching the throne:
we have a Priest
who is there interceding,
pouring his grace
on our lives day by day.[1]

Several years ago I went through a time of suffering from severe depression. During this period I continued to attend the Ministers' Conference of the group of churches to which our church belongs. I both looked and felt extremely ill. Several years later a fellow minister, who I did not know at all well, told me about the burden the Lord had given him to pray for me in this period. I was very touched by this and thought of how the Lord had used this friend's prayers to bring subsequent blessing into my life. On one level the encouragement about Christ's intercession is simply this; someone has been praying and is praying for us. Past blessings and the hope of future blessings relate to this. However, because of who Jesus is, his intercession surpasses any intercession we may make for each other. In this chapter we will continue to look at the way in which the writer to the Hebrews seeks to encourage his readers through his teaching on Christ's intercession. We will also examine points concerning the relationship between Christ's intercession and our praying, and concerning the Holy Spirit in the book of Hebrews. We will then go on, in the next chapter, to examine the gospel accounts of Jesus' praying to see what pattern Jesus established on earth for his heavenly ministry of intercession.

Encouragements drawn from Christ's intercession

The main texts dealing with this are Hebrews 4:14–16, Hebrews 7:25–26 and Hebrews 10:19–25. It is important to realize that to look to them for encouragement, in the broadest sense, is to understand them properly. The writer to the Hebrews describes his letter as 'my word of exhortation [encouragement]'(Hebrews 13:22). In reading Hebrews we should realize that first and foremost we are dealing with a message of encouragement, with meaty doctrinal sections, rather than a doctrinal treatise with added on applications. This orientation is vital in enabling us to remain on track when faced with some of the complexities of the book.

WHAT IT MEANS TO US TO HAVE A FAITHFUL AND SYMPATHETIC HIGH PRIEST

Therefore, since we have a great high priest who has gone through the heavens, Jesus the Son of God, let us hold firmly to the faith we profess. For we do not have a high priest who is unable to sympathise with our weakness, but we have one who has been tempted in every way, just as we are—yet was without sin. Let us then approach the throne of grace with confidence, so that we may receive mercy and find grace to help us in our time of need.(Hebrews 4:14–16)

We need to remind ourselves of the situation of temptation these Hebrew Christians were in. Their major temptation was to let go of the faith they had professed and, most probably, to return to the fold of Jewish nation and faith. The writer has challenged them to realize that to win through to God's rest, consummated and fulfilled salvation, they must continue in their faith (3:14–15). He has warned them that their predecessors, the Hebrew nation delivered from Egypt, failed here through failure to continue in the faith (4:1–2). They are now facing the knife-edge of God's word (4:12–13)—will they continue in faith or will they drop out?

The section began with a call to 'fix your thoughts on Jesus, the apostle and high priest whom we confess. He was faithful ...' (3:1). It is to this theme of faithfulness we return in our text, for the encouragement to, 'hold firmly to the faith we profess' is based on Jesus' faithfulness under temptation. The line of thought is:'—

1 Jesus has been faithful under pressure to abandon his obedience to God.

2 This means that he has fully experienced temptation and can sympathise with us in our temptations.

3 The fact that he has successfully dealt with temptation means he has now gone, in his human nature, and with all his human experience, into God's presence as 'a great High Priest'.

4 As our, 'great high priest' he assures us that we can continually enter God's presence 'with confidence' and receive 'mercy and grace to help us in our time of need' from one who feels our situation with us.

5 This assurance of help means we can continue in 'the faith we profess'.

The first three points have all been dealt with in chapters 4, 5 and 6 and we will restrict our attention to points four and five.

THE CHRISTIAN'S CONFIDENCE

The 'confidence' we are to have relates to our right to be there in God's presence whenever we need or desire to draw near to him. Whatever we may have done and however we may have been tempted to backslide and abandon our faith we have a perfect right to draw near to God. Andrew Bonar puts this very quaintly:

Suppose that I, a sinner, be walking along yon golden street, passing one angel after another. I can hear them say as I pass through their ranks, 'A sinner! [3] a crimson sinner!' Should my feet totter? Should my eye grow dim? No; I can say to them, 'Yes a sinner, a crimson sinner, but a sinner brought near by a forsaken Saviour, and now a sinner who has boldness [confidence NIV] to enter into the Holiest through the blood of Jesus.' [2]

The confidence that we have in drawing near also extends to the fact that we expect to 'receive mercy and find grace to help us in our time of need.' God will forgive us our sins and will provide the grace we need at the present moment to deal with the temptations and difficulties that belong to this unique period in our lives. Jesus feels our situation with us and will grant us appropriate help. The bottom line is always that we will receive whatever we need in order to continue in the faith. The Hebrew Christians will have been very aware that, for their old covenant counterparts, every wilderness need had been supplied. God calls us to the genuine confidence in God that our needs will be supplied. Donald Guthrie writes: 'The supply of grace is unrestricted, the only condition being a willingness to receive it, a sense of its indispensability.'4 So the presence of Jesus in heaven as our 'great High Priest' guarantees we will receive acceptance, understanding and appropriate help as we draw near in prayer to God. Hence we will be enabled to continue strongly and confidently as those publicly committed to the Christian faith.

WHAT IT MEANS TO HAVE CHRIST CONSTANTLY INTERCEDING FOR US

'Therefore he is able to save completely those who come to God through him, because he always lives to intercede for them. Such a high priest meets our need' (Hebrews 7:25–26). In chapter three we considered Jesus' appointment by God as a High Priest in the order of Melchizedek. There were several points of superiority based on the new high priest's appointment by oath, permanency and sinlessness. The superiority, as we experience it, is that 'such a high priest meets our need' and that we have through him 'a better hope … by which we draw near to God' (7:19). The need we have is that we can draw near to God, that we can know our sins are forgiven and that we are assured of all the help we need for our earthly pilgrimage.

We have already pointed out that the word translated 'completely' brings with it the idea expressed in the NIV margin of 'for ever.' So we understand the verse as saying that Jesus is able to save completely and for ever those who come to God through him. John Owen writes that after our first experience of salvation:

There may great oppositions be made against it, in temptations, trials, sins, and death, before it be brought into perfection; but our Lord Christ, as our faithful high priest, fainteth not in his work, but is able to carry us through all these difficulties, and will do so, until it be finished for ever in heaven … He is able to save completely as to all parts, fully as to all causes, and for ever in duration. … [therefore] Whatever hindrances and difficulties lie in the way of the salvation of believers, whatever oppositions do rise against it, the Lord Christ is able, by virtue of his sacerdotal [priestly] office, and in the exercise of it, to carry the work through them all unto eternal perfection.5

The result then of considering this truth should be a renewed confidence not just about our current acceptance by God but also our continuing persevering in faith. Wayne Grudem writes:

The thought that Jesus is continually praying for us should give us great encouragement. He always prays for us according to the Father's will, so we can know his requests will be granted. Berkhof says: 'It is a consoling thought that Christ is praying for us, even when we are negligent in our prayer life; that He is presenting to the Father those spiritual needs which were not present to our minds and which we often neglect to include in our prayers; and that He prays for our protection against the dangers of which we are not even conscious, and against the enemies which threaten us, though we do not notice it. He is praying that our faith may not cease, and that we may come out victoriously in the end.'[6]

Comforting though this is when we are repentantly considering our negligence in our commitment to Christian living and prayer, the pastoral intention of the writer to the Hebrews is not to comfort us in our negligence but to stimulate us to renewed faithfulness.

However many situations occur when it is not possible for us to pray, as we need to. We may be ignorant of situations and impending temptations of which our Saviour is aware and for which he is able to intercede effectively. As happened to a member of my congregation recently, we may be mentally affected by an accident or medical condition and so unable to pray. In such a situation it is a comfort that when we cannot pray at all, let alone pray as we should, that someone else is interceding effectively for us. The same comfort should help us in facing old age with its danger of the possible loss of mental alertness and clarity and even of developing dementia. In all situations it is a comfort for us to realize that Christ's intercession is based on superior knowledge and wisdom concerning our needs.

THE RESPONSIBILITIES OF HAVING A GREAT HIGH PRIEST

[19]Therefore brothers, since we have confidence to enter the Most Holy Place by the blood of Jesus, [20]by a new and living way opened for us through the curtain, that is, his body, [21]and since we have a great priest over the house of God, [22]let us draw near to God with a sincere heart in full assurance of faith, having our hearts sprinkled to

cleanse us from a guilty conscience and having our bodies washed with pure water. ²³Let us hold unswervingly to the hope we profess, for he who promised is faithful. ²⁴And let us consider how we may spur one another on towards love and good deeds. ²⁵Let us not give up meeting together, as some are in the habit of doing, but let us encourage one another—and all the more as you see the Day approaching. (Hebrews 10:19–25)

Verses 19–23 largely repeat what has been expounded already and therefore we will confine our study to vs 24 and 25. These bring in the important dimension of our responsibilities to our fellow believers.

It is fair to say here that many evangelicals have suffered from short-sightedness, sometimes even amounting to blindness, in their reading of Scripture on this point. One prominent 19th century evangelical was described as belonging to a school of thought who 'had no conception at all of the church idea. They were gospel preachers seeking only to evoke individual experience ... they were individualists of the most marked type.'[7] Hebrews, like all other scriptures, is not addressed to the individual believer but to the Christian community and to individuals as community members. Therefore to respond appropriately to the high priesthood of Jesus will affect our attitudes in the community of God's people as well as our own devotional life.

One attitude that the New Testament writers would find utterly alien is the one that says, 'I am not committed to any particular church because that doesn't really matter—what is important is that I'm a member of the Universal Church.' Rick Warren in his book: *The Purpose Driven Church* points out that nearly every Christian knows John 3:16[8] but very few know 1 John 3:16[9] (see the footnotes if you don't!). In the New Testament all Christians are members of local assemblies and their obedience to the New Testament commands can only take place within the local assembly where they have committed relationships to other people. There are actually over fifty commands in the New Testament regarding our relationships and responsibilities to 'each other/one another.' As John Piper expresses it: 'Perseverance in faith is a community project'.[10]

Hebrews is no exception to this New Testament perspective. In vs 19–22 the readers are urged to have confident and believing fellowship with God through Jesus. In v 23 they are urged to hold to the faith without faltering or swerving aside. In vs 24–25 we see that the responsibility to ensure continuance in the faith is not merely individual but communal. The accent here is on helping positive progress rather than the earlier warning emphasis of 3:12–13, 'See to it, brothers, that none of you has a sinful, unbelieving heart that turns away from the living God. But encourage one another daily, as long as it is called Today, so that none of you may be hardened by sin's deceitfulness.' Here the stress is to 'spur one another on to love and good deeds' and to continue 'meeting together.' Clearly the fear of persecution, plus a falling away in their appreciation of God's love for them, had led to both a decrease in meeting together for fellowship and in a weakening of the mutual love that existed between them. Nowadays, some Christians justify withdrawing from regularly meeting together with other Christians on the basis that they can continue their fellowship with God without having fellowship with other believers. This is really self-deception of a very dangerous variety. It is not that we want to say that a Christian in a Robinson Crusoe situation, or in solitary confinement, could not be sustained by God—clearly they could be. Rather it is voluntary spiritual isolationism that is to be seen as spiritually wrong and dangerous. I can remember this spiritual syndrome being bluntly described by Douglas McMillan, who was a former shepherd turned preacher: 'The sheep that doesn't want to be with other sheep' he said, 'is sick!' Donald Guthrie is equally clear, though less colourful: 'The New Testament lends no support to the idea of lone Christians. Close and regular fellowship with other believers is not just a nice idea, but an absolute necessity for the encouragement of Christian values.'[11]

If you are suffering from this sickness, described in Revelation 2:4 as having 'forsaken your first love', then you need to seek recovery. This comes by a rekindled sense of God's love in Christ and by being prepared to 'Repent and do the things you did at first' (Revelation 2:5). This emphasis carries the Hebrew Christians back to their early days where they stood firm under temptation and 'stood side by side with those who were so treated. [and] You sympathised with those in prison' (Hebrews 10:33–34). By example and by word of mouth they are to help one another regain that love and mutual commitment.

They are to do this, 'all the more as you see the Day approaching.' Clearly the persecution and isolation felt by them had diminished their belief that God would intervene to help them in their present situation. With that diminution of belief also went a failing faith in 'the glorious appearing of our great God and Saviour, Jesus Christ' (Titus 2:13) which is the great intervention of God in Christ to save us for ever. This did not mean that the Hebrew Christians would have said that Jesus was not coming again. What it did mean was that this hope that Christians all share had become weak and that their lives were not governed and controlled by their faith. However now their faith in Jesus' sympathy and ability to help them had been renewed so also the blessed hope resumed its rightful place in their expectations.

Christ's intercession and our own prayers

Quite clearly Christ's intercession is not seen as a substitute for our praying which would render our own praying useless. The relationship between his praying and our praying is very similar to the relationship between God working and our endeavour in the matter of sanctification. This is expressed succinctly for us in Philippians 2:12–13, 'continue to work out your salvation with fear and trembling, for it is God who works in you to will and to act according to his good purpose.' Here it is not that God works, and therefore we do not need to, or that we are left to do it all with God as an onlooker. Rather we work, with confidence, because God is working. In the same way we pray, with confidence, because Christ is already interceding. This means I will not give up with my praying because I think, 'I do not need to bother with prayer because Jesus is praying for me.' It means I will not give up praying because I am driven to despair by the feeling that everything is down to me, and to my self-discipline, and that this enterprise of prayer is clearly unrealistic and will inevitably fail. It means I will pray because I am strengthened by the confidence that my prayers accompany and are upheld by the praying of my Saviour.

This perspective, that we pray because Jesus is praying, is a perspective that many writers on prayer have picked up. Calvin writes about our perspective on the relationship of our prayers and Christ's intercession: 'All our prayers should be founded on the intercession of Christ.'[12] John Owen writes: 'And the incense which he offereth with the prayers of the saints,

Revelation 8:3–4, is no other but his own intercession, whereby their prayers are made acceptable unto God.'[13] Douglas Kelly writes of our involvement in intercession: 'When we commit ourselves to stand "in the gap" we find that he is already there in the place of intercession. We are actually joining him who is our life and strength.'[14] More poetically James Montgomery wrote:

> Nor prayer is made on earth alone;
> The Holy Spirit pleads;
> And Jesus on the eternal throne,
> For sinners intercedes.[15]

So when we turn to pray, and often find concentration and clarity of thought hard to come by, we are to be helped by the truth that our weak prayers are taken up into our glorified Saviour's life of intercession.

The Holy Spirit in Hebrews

In considering the encouragements that we receive through the intercession of Christ we move on to make a general point. Strangely the book of Hebrews is very sparse in its references to the Holy Spirit. None of the references there are take up the subject of the Spirit's role in enabling our sanctification and perseverance in the Christian life. Far from being an omission this seems to be a deliberate policy on the writer's part and is designed to focus attention on Jesus and his ability to help. HH Meeter reflects insightfully on this:

Had the fact received due consideration, that the Holy Spirit is now sent into the church as the Spirit of the Son, being so closely related to him as to enable Paul to say: 'The Lord is the Spirit' (2 Corinthians 3:17), then the truth, that the application of the work of redemption in sanctification is the direct work of the heavenly High Priest through his Spirit, would have accordingly been placed in the foreground, and the need for the Christian to go constantly to the High Priest in heaven for aid would have received a corresponding emphasis.[16]

The same Spirit who indwelt and enabled the Son's obedience is sent, with that experience and knowledge of human temptation and need, into our hearts to help us on our road to holiness.

Moving on

In the next chapter we will examine the relevance of the pattern of intercession Jesus established on earth to our understanding of his present intercession for us.

Notes

1 **Wendy Churchill,** *Jesus is King and I will extol Him*, Springtide/Word Music (UK), copyright 1981.

2 **Andrew Bonar,** *Heavenly Springs*, original publication 1904, Banner of Truth, edition 1986, p. 175.

3 Isaiah 1:18.

4 **Donald Guthrie,** *Tyndale New Testamentary Commentary on Hebrews,* IVP, 1983, p. 124.

5 **John Owen,** *Exposition of Hebrews—volume 5*, Baker Book House, p. 529.

6 **Wayne Grudem,** *Systematic Theology*, IVP, 1994, p. 628 quoting **Louis Berkhof,** *Systematic Theology*, Banner of Truth, 1958, p. 403.

7 **Marcus Rainsford,** *Our Lord Prays for His Own*, Moody Press, 1978. In S Maxwell Coder's biographical introduction Rainsford is so described (possibly unfairly) by his high church Son William.

8 'For God so loved the world that he gave his one and only Son, that whoever believes in him shall not perish but have eternal life.'

9 'This is how we know what love is: Jesus Christ laid down his life for us. And we ought to lay down our lives for our brothers.'

10 **John Piper,** *A Godward Life*, Kingsway, 1998, p. 189.

11 **Donald Guthrie,** *op. cit.,* p. 216.

12 **Graham Miller,** *Calvin's Wisdom*, Banner of Truth, 1992, p. 173.

13 **John Owen,** *op. cit.,* p. 539.

14 **Douglas Kelly,** *If God Already Knows, Why Pray?*, Wolgemuth and Hyatt, 1989, p. 189.

15 **James Montgomery,** *Prayer is the soul's sincere desire.*

16 **HH Meeter,** *The Heavenly High Priesthood of Christ*, Eerdmans, pp. 206–7.

Christ's intercession (3)

Awake, sweet gratitude and sing
The ascended Saviour's love:
Sing how he lives to carry on
His people's cause above.

With cries and tears he offered up
His humble suit below;
But with authority he asks,
Enthroned in glory now.[1]

Jesus' earthly prayers illuminate his present intercession

In this chapter we are going to look at the way in which Jesus' earthly life and particularly his recorded prayers give us guidelines for how we are to understand his present intercession for us. It will be a tremendous help and inspiration for us to know what it is that Jesus is interceding for on our behalf in heaven.

There is however an obvious objection to this procedure, which we need to face. This is that there is so great a difference between Jesus in his humiliation on earth and his glorification in heaven that we cannot properly draw such inferences. The answer actually comes in what is probably the best known text from the book of Hebrews which is: 'Jesus Christ is the same yesterday and today and for ever' (13:8). He who (3:2) was faithful, 'yesterday' in his earthly life and to Christian leaders in the past (13:7) will certainly be faithful to you, 'today' and to those who follow you in the faith, 'for ever.' In other words the text is not abstractly about the essence and being of Christ but about his constancy, the fact that he will be 'the same', towards us and future believers as he has been to his followers in the past. Without the gospel records serving as a window onto Christ's present intercession we would be greatly handicapped in our appreciation and understanding of what it means to have him interceding for us.

Our treatment of this subject is not meant to be exhaustive but takes several passages which show us the Saviour in prayer for his people. The way in which we apply those passages to ourselves will encourage us to look to Jesus as interceding for us and enlighten us as to some of his concerns in that intercession.

Jesus' present intercession anticipated in the high priestly prayer

JC Ryle describes John 17 by saying: 'It is wonderful as a specimen of the communion that was kept up between the Father and the Son, during the period of the Son's ministry on earth—it is wonderful as a pattern of the intercession which the Son, as an high Priest, is ever carrying on for us in heaven.'[2] There are some aspects of the prayer that are outside our present concerns. For example vs 1–5 concern the Lord Jesus himself and his return to glory via the route of his death on the cross, his resurrection and ascension. Verses 6–19 are mainly to do with the disciples but some of this portion of the prayer may rightly be generalised to apply to his intercession for all his followers. Verses 20–26 apply directly to his intercession for us who are 'those who will believe in me through their [the disciples'] message' (v 20). William Milligan captures the spirit of Jesus' intercession in John 17 and its relevance to our present topic:

In heaven only is he perfect High-priest, and the words of the prayer belong at least in spirit to that upper sanctuary. They are the concentration of all the prayers of the heavenly Intercessor, as he bore on earth, as he bears now, and will bear for ever, the wants of his people before the Father, who is both able and willing to supply them.[3]

JESUS PRAYS FOR HIS DISCIPLES

A question that preachers sometimes ask is why, when we are saved, we are not whisked straight off to heaven, which is certainly a happier, and would seem to be a safer, place. The question is rhetorical and usually gets the answer: 'To witness.' Actually God's plan is greater than that (see

Ephesians 3:10–11). Here Jesus prays for his disciples to be protected: 'My prayer is not that you take them out of the world but that you protect them from the evil one. They are not of the world, even as I am not of it.' (John 17:15–16).

Because, like Jesus, the disciples are on God's side, rather than siding with a world hostile to God and his servants, Jesus prays for their protection. They are not to be taken out of the world, as Jesus will be when he returns to glory, but are to be protected as they remain in the world. DA Carson writes:

Doubtless Christians in John's day were forced to ponder the implications of this prayer. … The cosmic, spiritual nature of the conflict is laid bare. The followers of Jesus are permitted neither the luxury of compromise with a 'world' that is intrinsically evil and under the devil's power, nor the safety of disengagement. But if the Christian pilgrimage is inherently perilous, the safety that only God himself can provide is assured, as certainly as the prayers of God's own dear Son will be answered.4

As we battle on in the Christian life, and often feel very insecure and weak and frightened at the extent of opposition we face, we need to have something of the conviction of the hymn-writer who wrote:

Yes, I to the end shall endure,
As sure as the earnest is given;
More happy, but not more secure,
The glorified spirits in heaven.5

'Sanctify them by the truth; your word is truth. As you have sent me into the world, I have sent them into the world. For them I sanctify myself, that they too may be truly sanctified' (John 17:17–19)

What is your idea of a 'sanctified' person? I guess that often the mental picture conjured up is one of withdrawal to a contemplative life, summed up for me in the monk's quarters at Mount Grace Priory in North Yorkshire, where the monks all had a kind of private bed-sit for reading and contemplation, where even the meals were served so that monk and servitor had no contact. However attractive this may be, it is not what Jesus has in mind in his prayer.

DA Carson comments:

In John's Gospel, such 'sanctification' is always for mission. Jesus is both set apart and, 'sent' by the Father and sets himself apart for the Father's service. This is done so that it may impact on his followers and their lives. ... Jesus dedicates himself to the task of bringing in God's saving reign, as God's priest and prophet; but the purpose of this dedication is that his followers may dedicate themselves to the same saving reign, the same mission to the world (v 18).[6]

So we are not to view our salvation as culminating in our own 'Safety, Certainty and Enjoyment'[7] but in serving God's intention to bless a sinful, rebellious world through his Son and his Son's followers. Activity in evangelism and Christian service is not an alternative to sanctification but how sanctification is to be worked out. We are sanctified as we respond to all God's truth (v 17), not just to those parts which we regard as relating to the 'spiritual life.'

JESUS PRAYS FOR ALL BELIEVERS AT ALL TIMES

The main objects of his prayer are their unity (vs 20–23) and that they may be able to see his own glory (vs 24–26). With this goes knowledge of God's love for them and Jesus' presence with them.

A PRAYER FOR UNITY

[20]'I pray also ...[21]that all of them may be one, Father, just as you are in me and I am in you. May they also be in us so that the world may believe that you have sent me. [22]I have given them the glory that you gave me, that they may be one as we are one: [23]I in them and you in me. May they be brought to complete unity to let the world know that you sent me and have loved them even as you have loved me.' (John 17:20–23)

Clearly the focus of the unity that Jesus prays for is not institutional and organisational. It is a unity based on the relationship between Father and Son, 'just as you are in me and I am in you' (v 21) and the relationship between the Trinity and believers (vs 21–23), 'may they also be in us ... that they may be one as we are one: I in them and you in me.' Calvin explains our oneness with Christ as being saving rather than mystical: 'by the power of the Spirit he communicates to us his life and all the blessings he has received from the Father.'[8] In line with this insight, DA Carson expresses the unity that is prayed for as: 'sharing richly in the community of purpose and the wealth of love that tie the Father and the Son together.'[9]

Though the unity prayed for is not institutional it is certainly observable. Through it 'the world may believe that you have sent me' (v 21) and, 'the world [can] know that you have loved them even as you have loved me.' Evangelism depends for its credibility on the life of the Christian community displaying God's love. How is this to be done and what actions should we be involved with to enable this to be so? Schemes for church unity soar over the head of most ministers as well as other Christians. The reality of this prayer is more down to earth and in our own hands than this, because it concerns the local assembly of God's people.

Consider this story about a first generation Jamaican immigrant:

Aunt Liza came to this country in 1956. She was told by her minister in Jamaica to make sure that she found her way to the Methodist Church when she arrived in London. She did just that. On the first Sunday that she was in London, she put on her best hat and went to the Methodist Church, which her landlady had pointed out to her. When the minister came into the church to start the service, he looked down from the pulpit and saw Aunt Liza. He came down the aisle, escorted her to the church door and said, 'Your church is just down the road there.'[10]

Hopefully nowadays we would not be guilty of crass racism like that. However I wonder if we see the issue of unity across racial, cultural and other barriers as a gospel issue, an issue relating to the true meaning and mandatory implications of the gospel. Whether we see that an observable unity, which crosses such barriers as race and culture, is vital to showing the validity of the gospel we preach.

Our church, which is a small inner-city church in an industrial town in the North-East, has in recent years had people attending from the Congo, Sierra Leone, Nigeria, Rwanda, Burundi, Angola, the Ivory Coast, Taiwan, Malaysia, Hong-Kong, Iran, France, Holland, Australia, Wales, Ireland

and Scotland. Plus we have had others who are second generation immigrants from Egypt and Bangladesh. The diversity denominationally and theologically is almost as great; Baptists (some strongly Calvinistic and some not), Presbyterians, Dutch Reformed, Nazarenes, Anglicans, Pentecostals, Methodists and Charismatics—and we are actually an Evangelical Congregational Church! It is all too easy to give the non-verbal message that only people of our sort are wanted here. It is not that our church has no theological or ecclesiological convictions, but rather that one of our major convictions is that when Christians will commit themselves to the church and its ministry, it is our duty to seek to hold together in unity with them.

This is not always easy—we have not even mentioned the existence of personality differences! It is certainly easy enough to feel that genuine congregational unity is unattainable. What a challenge to know that our gospel credibility rests on this unity and what a comfort to know that our Saviour's intercession undergirds and enables it! So whenever you feel like giving up on the church, or giving in to the temptation to be disagreeable to, and dismissive of other Christians, remember Jesus is praying for you, and with you, for unity.

A PRAYER THAT HIS FOLLOWERS MAY SEE HIS GLORY

24'Father, I want those you have given me to be with me where I am, and to see my glory, the glory you have given me because you loved me before the creation of the world. 25Righteous Father, though the world does not know you, I know you, and they know that you have sent me. 26I have made you known to them, and will continue to make you known in order that the love you have for me may be in them and that I myself may be in them' (John 17:24–26).

In this prayer there is both an ultimate goal and a short-term goal for, 'those you have given me' (v 24) who consist of God's elect, being both the disciples and those who follow in their footsteps of faith.

The short-term goal—or the goal which relates most fully to their life on earth and enables the ultimate goal—is that 'the love you have for me may be in them and that I myself may be in them' (v 26). DA Carson writes:

The crucial point is that this text does not simply make these followers the objects of God's love, but promises that they will be so transformed as God is continually being made known to them, that God's own love for his Son will become their love. The love with which they learn to love is nothing less than the love amongst the persons of the Godhead.[11]

However this experience and living out of a life of love on earth is not the ultimate goal for a Christian. The Christian's ultimate goal is to be with Christ where he now is (v 24) and there to see his glory. Calvin writes:

At that time they saw Christ's glory as a man shut up in the dark obtains a feeble half-light through small crevices. Christ now wishes that they should go on to enjoy the full brightness of heaven. In short, he asks that the Father will lead them by uninterrupted progress to the full view of his glory.[12]

Currently we are aware that whatever we may have experienced spiritually we are only like those who 'see but a poor reflection as in a mirror' (1 Corinthians 13:12). However, we will see 'face to face' and 'be like him, for we shall see him as he is' (1 John 3:2).

There is something very emphatic about the language used by Jesus in his prayer 'I want ...' (v 24), which I think fits with the point that: 'God's [will or desire] is characterised by definiteness, assurance and efficacy.'[13] Clearly there is no thought at all of refusal of the prayer. Again we are being assured that Christ's continued intercession in heaven will ensure that we will be growing in the experience and expression of God's love and that we may be absolutely confident of seeing the glory of Jesus. As we find it hard to continue a life of love, facing discouragements and hurts, and as we struggle onwards it is wonderful to reflect that our certainty of glory rests on Jesus' certainty of answered prayer.

Jesus' intercession for Peter

Uniquely in Luke's gospel we have not only Jesus' warning to Simon Peter that he will deny him three times but also his assurance that he has prayed for him: 'Simon, Simon, Satan has asked to sift you [plural, meaning all the disciples] as wheat. But I have prayed for you, Simon [singular, meaning

Simon as an individual], that your faith may not fail. And when you have
turned back, strengthen your brothers' (Luke 22:31–32).
The situation envisaged is one of severe testing:

The sifting of wheat basically refers to the repeated, swift and violent shaking of the
wheat in a sieve. Someone ... grasps the sieve in both hands, and begins to shake
vigorously from side to side so that the chaff will rise to the surface. This then is thrown
away. Next, she puts that sieve through a teeter-totter motion, raising now this, and
then that side, and blowing over it, so that what still remains of the chaff gathers in an
easily removable pile.[14]

Without pressing the details of the illustration we can see that this is a vivid
metaphor for a period of testing which will severely test the faith of the
disciples. While all the disciples are prayed for in John 17:6–19, Peter has a
particular assurance that the Lord Jesus has prayed for him directly and
personally. Once again the prayer by Jesus guarantees its answer will be
forthcoming, for it is 'when [not 'if'] you have turned back' (v 32).

The message of this story to its first readers is clear. They were faced
with persecution and possible martyrdom as was almost universal, from
time to time, with the early church. 'Luke in this account revealed to his
disciples that prayer was the means by which Peter and the disciples were
kept from falling away from the faith. Because Jesus prayed, Peter's failure
did not end in apostasy.'[15] For Christians who are overwhelmed by
pressures against them and tempted to fall away, or for those who have
already denied Christ under pressure from the authorities, it is a
tremendous comfort that their continuance in the faith depends on Jesus'
faithful prayer and not primarily on the strength of their own faithfulness.
JC Ryle writes:

The continued existence of grace in a believer's heart is a great standing miracle. His
enemies are so mighty, and his strength so small, the world is so full of snares, and his
heart so weak, that it seems at first sight impossible for him to reach heaven. The
passage before us explains his safety: he has a mighty Friend at the right hand of God,
who ever lives to make intercession for him; there is a watchful Advocate, who is daily
pleading for him, seeing all his daily necessities, and obtaining daily supplies of mercy

and grace for his soul. His grace never altogether dies, because Christ always lives to intercede.[16]

The community emphasis of that we have already found in Hebrews is also present here, because Peter is told to, 'strengthen your brothers' (v 32). Robert H Stein writes: 'In the New Testament this verb frequently describes the process of helping someone grow in the Christian faith.'[17] So the whole task of encouraging, leading and teaching is open to those who may for a while have faltered in their faith. It is open to those who have faltered because Jesus has not faltered in praying for them.

Jesus sends help to his disciples

Immediately Jesus made his disciples get into the boat and go on ahead of him to Bethsaida, while he dismissed the crowd. After leaving them, he went up on a mountainside to pray.

When evening came, the boat was in the middle of the lake, and he was alone on land. He saw the disciples straining at the oars, because the wind was against them. About the fourth watch of the night he went out to them, walking on the lake. He was about to pass by them, but when they saw him walking on the lake, they thought he was a ghost. They cried out, because they all saw him and were terrified.

Immediately he spoke to them and said, 'Take courage! It is I. Don't be afraid.' Then he climbed into the boat with them, and the wind died down. They were completely amazed, for they had not understood about the loaves; their hearts were hardened. (Mark 6:45–52)

Jesus sends his disciples ahead of him to Bethsaida. From the emphasis that, 'Jesus made his disciples get into the boat' (v 45) we gather that, like the death of Jesus and his departure into heaven, this was not at all welcome to them. Without him they struggle, 'straining at the oars, because the wind was against them' (v 48). WL Lane describes a recurring pattern in Mark's gospel: 'Whenever the master is absent from the disciples (or appears to be so …) they find themselves in distress. And each time they experience anguish it is because they lack faith.'[18] This is a situation every subsequent generation of believers can identify with and are intended to identify with.

The reality of course is that Jesus is praying, 'he went up on a mountainside to pray' (v 46) and aware of their situation, 'He saw the disciples straining at the oars, because the wind was against them' (v 48). This is clearly supernatural because although he has a vantage point (v 46) it is 3am, 'the fourth watch of the night' (v 48), and he would not be able to see them in the darkness before the dawn. His response to their need is to come to them and to control their situation for them. WL Lane writes: 'At an early date this episode was interpreted as a pledge of Christ's aid; it provided the martyrs with the assurance of Jesus' saving nearness to all who believe and obey him.'[19]

It does also of course convey the message, that, in all our distresses, and whenever we feel that Jesus is far from us, we need not despair. The reality is that we are seen by him, we are the objects of his prayers and will soon be the recipients of his help. Andrew Bonar puts it in a characteristically quaint way:

When we are united to Christ we can say, 'I am in Christ,' as well as, 'Christ is in me.' My faith need have no ups and downs, for my righteousness is in heaven. I may lose my sight of it, but it is there all the same. There is the boat on the Lake of Galilee. Dark night is coming on, and the disciples are in danger. Let us suppose two angels are looking on, and one says, 'There are the Master's disciples, and they are in sore trouble.' 'There is no fear,' the other says. 'They are the Master's property. He is in the mountain praying for them.' In a little while they can see the Master leave the mountain, walk over the sea, and come into the boat. 'Ah,' they say, 'it is impossible they can sink now. He is in the boat with them.'[20]

Conclusion

It is very clear that from the earliest days of the Christian church, before even the gospels were written, the believers were taught the words and told the stories of Jesus. As we come to understand the priesthood and intercession of Jesus, it illuminates gospel stories for us and reminds us that Jesus is even now praying for us. Even now he is praying for us in temptation and danger and coming to us to help in time of need.

Chapter 10

Moving on

We have now completed our examination of the priesthood and intercession of Christ as explained for us in the book of Hebrews and as anticipated in the gospels. As with all generations of Christians we come to these great truths with the particular pressures and temptations of our own situation in history. In that sense faith is never second-hand and is always to be practised in the existential moment in which we live. As the writer to the Hebrews puts it, 'Today, if you hear his voice, do not harden your hearts ...' (Hebrews 3:15 quoting Psalm 95:7–8) However countless generations of believers have experienced crises of faith and have found comfort in the same truths. It is to the experience of earlier generations of believers that we now turn.

Notes

1 **AM Toplady,** *Awake sweet gratitude and sing.*
2 **JC Ryle,** *Expository Thoughts on the Gospels (John)* Vol. III, James Clark and Co., 1957, p. 188.
3 **William Milligan,** *The Ascension and Heavenly Priesthood of Our Lord,* MacMillan and Co., 1908, p. 156.
4 **DA Carson,** *The Gospel according to John,* IVP, 1991, p. 565.
5 **Augustus Montague Toplady,** *A Debtor to Mercy alone.*
6 **DA Carson,** *op. cit.,* pp. 566–567.
7 The title of a well-known tract.
8 **John Calvin,** *John's Gospel 11–21 and 1 John*, St Andrew Press, 1961, p. 148.
9 **DA Carson,** *op. cit.,* p. 569.
10 **Eddie Gibbs** (ed), *Ten Growing Churches,* Marc Europe, 1984, pp. 32–33.
11 **DA Carson,** *op. cit.,* p. 570.
12 **John Calvin,** *op. cit.,* pp. 150–151.
13 **KL Schmidt** in Kittel and Friedrich, *Theological Dictionary of the New Testament,* (one volume), Eerdmans, 1985, p. 318.
14 **William Hendriksen,** *New Testament Commentary on Luke,* Banner of Truth, 1979, p. 973.
15 **Robert H Stein,** *The New American Commentary on Luke*, Broadman Press, 1992, p. 553.
16 **JC Ryle,** *Expository Thoughts on the Gospels, (Luke)* (Volume 2), William Hunt and Co., 1874, p. 411.

17 Robert H Stein, *op. cit.,* p. 553.
18 William L Lane, *New International Commentary on Mark*, Eerdmans, 1974, p. 235.
19 William L Lane, *op. cit.,* p. 239.
20 Andrew Bonar, *Heavenly Springs*, first published 1904, Banner of Truth, 1986, p. 68.

Witnesses from the past

Therefore, since we are surrounded by such a great cloud of witnesses, let us throw off everything that hinders and the sin that so easily entangles, and let us run with perseverance the race marked out for us. Let us fix our eyes on Jesus, the author and perfecter of our faith, who for the joy set before him endured the cross, scorning its shame, and sat down at the right hand of the throne of God.[1]

In one sense we could say that we have now fully explored the subject of Jesus as our Great High Priest, one who sympathises for us and has an ongoing ministry of intercession for us. However, truly to understand the gospel does not stop at intellectual enlightenment. God's truth as given in the gospel is always 'the truth that leads to godliness' (Titus 1:1). Like the other New Testament writers, the writer to the Hebrews urges his readers to practical, spiritual response to his teaching. He is concerned to show that God has blessed and honoured those who have lived by faith in his word in previous generations, so that his readers will do the same in their generation. In Hebrews, a clear contrast can be drawn between the writer's teaching on salvation history, where he emphasizes the development between the two covenants, and on faith, where he emphasizes the continuity of faith within the covenant community.[2] As regards the life of faith he teaches direct lessons from the lives of old covenant believers—both as regards the trials and the triumphs of their faith.

There is however an unavoidable difficulty the writer faces. None of those whom he will write about in Hebrews 11 were actually responding to the truths concerning Jesus as our High Priest. Although he shows the relevance of his Old Testament examples of faith to those of us following in their footsteps we have an advantage that he did not have. Living at this stage of the new covenant era we have the examples of many generations of believers who have lived by faith in these truths. We share both our faith and our great High Priest with every previous generation of Christians. They too have taken hold of these truths and have made them their own and benefited from them when faced with the perennial temptation to give up and to compromise the faith. As we look back at those who suffered for the faith and those who faced martyrdom during the Protestant Reformation, and to those in countries like Cambodia, Indonesia and Iran who have endured similar experiences in the 20th and 21st centuries, we are encouraged to continue firm in our own faith.

In this chapter we will look in detail at just two instances of how these great truths have been used in the worship and devotion of the Lord's people. In both case the writers have clearly first received blessing for themselves, and have then turned their own blessings into encouraging and constructive devotional material to benefit others.

Focusing on the heart of Hebrews

In looking back at the experiences of past believers, we will not be dealing with every aspect of the book of Hebrews' teaching on Christ as our great High Priest. Rather we will follow the emphases we have followed so far in this book and focus on his empathy with us, and his intercession for us. These themes form the distinctive contribution and the heart of the letter to the Hebrews. It would be possible to survey widely for these themes in Christian devotional writing but I want to select just two outstandingly helpful items from the past—one to highlight Christ's empathy with us, and the other to focus on his intercession for us. In each case the background of the writer, both theologically and historically, will almost certainly be very different from our own—as may their way of expressing themselves. However, there is timelessness about real spiritual truth and experience and this makes their words speak to our depths.

CHRIST'S SYMPATHY FOR HIS PEOPLE

The first item comes from Joseph Hart (1712–68), who was a very highly regarded hymn-writer amongst the Calvinistic Independents and Baptists of the 18th Century. His popularity has continued in rather restricted circles to this day. His hymn writing highlights both deep doctrine and genuine Christian experience. He shows a rich appreciation of how Christ's sympathy springs from his true humanity and his experience of suffering:

A Man there is, a real Man,
With wounds still gaping wide,
From which rich streams of blood once ran,
In hands, and feet, and side.

'Tis no wild fancy of our brains,
No metaphor we speak;
The same dear Man in heaven now reigns,
That suffered for our sake.

This wondrous Man of whom we tell,
Is true Almighty God;
He bought our souls from death and hell
The price, His own heart's blood.

That human heart He still retains,
Though throned in highest bliss;
And feels each tempted member's pains
For our affliction's His.

Come then, repenting sinner, come;
Approach with humble faith:
Owe what thou wilt, the total sum
Is cancelled by His death!

His blood can cleanse the blackest soul;
And wash our guilt away.
He will present us sound and whole
In that tremendous day.

Christ's intercession for his people

Here we turn to an unknown writer from, I guess, the 19th century. The poem is included in a long unavailable book: *The Theology of Prayer* by Benjamin Morgan Palmer (1818–1902) who was a Southern Presbyterian and ministered in New Orleans for nearly fifty years. Douglas Kelly discovered it for us and writes:

The unknown author is imagining what the Son says to the Father when a humble Christian, someone like you or me, brings a stumbling prayer to the heavenly throne. Yes, we have sinned. Yes, we do not know how to pray, as we should. But Jesus is standing in the gap for us and with us. He is the secret source of our own strength to struggle through to victory in the mighty battle of intercession.

The Intercessor

Father, I bring this worthless child to thee,
To claim thy pardon once, yet once again.
Receive him at my hands, for he is mine.
He is a worthless child; he owns his guilt.
Look not on him; he cannot bear thy glance.
Look thou on me; his vileness I will hide.
He pleads not for himself, he dares not plead.
His cause is mine, I am his Intercessor.

By each pure drop of blood I lost for him,
By all the sorrows graven on my soul,
By every wound I bear, I claim it due.
Father divine! I cannot have him lost.
He is a worthless soul, but he is mine.
Sin hath destroyed him; sin hath died in me.
Death hath pursued him; I have conquered death.
Satan hath bound him; Satan is my slave.

My Father! hear him now—not him, but me.

I would not have him lost for all the world
Thou for my glory hast ordain'd and made,
Because he is a poor and contrite child,
And all, his every hope, on me reclines.
I know my children, and I know him mine;
By all the tears he weeps upon my bosom,
By his full heart that beateth against mine.

I know him by his sighings and his prayers,
By his deep trusting love, which clings to me.
I could not bear to see him cast away,
Weak as he is, the weakest of my flock,
The one that grieves me most, that moves me least.

I measure not my love by his returns,
And though the stripes I send to speed him home
Drive him upon the instant from my breast,
Still he is mine; I drew him from the world;
He has no right, no home, but in my love.
Though earth and hell against his soul conspire,
I shield him, keep him, save him, we are one.[3]

Our response to the high priesthood of Christ

If you are a Christian, then you will know times when God seems far away and you long for someone who really understands your human heart, and understands what it is like to feel that temptation to sin which threatens to overwhelm and overthrow us. You should know from these pages that in Jesus you have a real human being in heaven on your behalf, who can understand your weaknesses and your experience of temptation: 'For we do not have a high priest who is unable to sympathise with our weaknesses, but we have one who has been tempted in every way, just as we are—yet was without sin' (Hebrews 4:15). However the Lord Jesus has triumphed in his own experience of weakness and temptation: 'During the days of Jesus' life on earth, he offered up prayers and petitions with loud cries and tears to the one who could save him from death, and he was heard because of his reverent submission. Although he was a son, he learned obedience from what he suffered and, once made perfect, he became the source of eternal salvation to all who obey him and was designated by God to be high priest in the order of Melchizedek' (Hebrews 5:7–10). As a result of these experiences then, Jesus has received the calling he has as High Priest who 'is able to save completely those who come to God through him, because he always lives to intercede for them' (Hebrews 7:25). Looking at the pattern the writer of Hebrews and the gospel writers give us of Jesus' intercession must make us realize that there is no spiritual need a Christian may have that lies outside the range of his praying for us.

Understanding brings with it responsibility and, as these great truths lay hold of us, we must in turn take up our own responsibility to encourage others with them. Many Christians are struggling not because they are turning in heart from the gospel but because they fail to understand the full riches of the gospel. As we deepen our understanding so in many ways, we will use every means to help other Christians—by spiritual conversation, lending good Christian books and encouraging Christians to attend churches where they will be taught faithfully. This is the least we can do after all our Lord has done for us.

O strengthen me, that, while I stand
Firm on the rock, and strong in Thee,
I may stretch out a loving hand
To wrestlers with the troubled sea.[4]

Notes

1 Hebrews 12:1–2.
2 See especially **G Hughes,** *Hebrews and Hermeneutics,* CUP, 1979.
3 **Douglas Kelly,** *If God Already Knows, Why Pray?,* **Wolgemuth and Hyatt,** 1989, pp. 189–190 (poem found in **B M Palmer,** *Theology of Prayer*).
4 **Frances Ridley Havergal,** *Lord, speak to me, that I may speak.*